UP THE TE[
Down Aston and Lozells
RONALD K. MOORE

*A fascinating account of life in the
back streets of Birmingham before, during
and after the first World War*

Westwood Press Publications

PRINT SHOP, 44 BOLDMERE ROAD, SUTTON COLDFIELD
WEST MIDLANDS TELEPHONE 021-354 5913

3

This Book is Dedicated with thanks to:

Albert Kendall
Kenneth Moore
Mrs G. Mason
Mr S Roberts
Mr L. Brown
Mr & Mrs David Fleming
Chas. Farrington
Mrs Margaret Eades
Mrs Norah Campbell
Mrs Laura Lyons

Mrs Ashby
Miss Dorothy Done
Mrs E. Mason
Dan Pawson
Mr J.S. Webb
Mrs G. Barker
Mr S. Cartwright
Roy Brittain
Mary Kendall-Lloyd
Mrs Olive Moore

and my wife Penny, who listened patiently to numerous drafts.

ISBN 0 948025 09 3

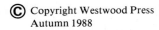
 Printed by The Westwood Press, 44 Boldmere Road
Sutton Coldfield. Produced by offset litho.

Contents

Victoria Road in the early 1900's

Six Ways, Aston, c. 1850

Six Ways, Aston looking down Birchfield Road with Lozells Road on the left and the
Midland Bank in the centre seen about sixty years later

6

Introduction

I WAS BORN in Birmingham in 1944 and am married with one married daughter.

My schooling was at King Edward's Camp Hill School, then Birmingham College of Art. During this time I made a photographic study of Aston, and in 1961 wrote a book on the early history of Birmingham for a thesis.

I then went on to Oxford College of Art and the Courtauld Institute of Art at London University, where I took an honours degree in the History of Art.

Initially I taught art and art history and then started a business in picture restoration, which I run from a smallholding on top of a mountain in mid Wales, near Lake Vyrnwy, where we keep goats, hens, two cats and a sheepdog called Meg.

Other publications include *Memories of Clun* — an account of Edwardian life in this small rural town in Shropshire, *Birmingham in Camera* — a photographic history of Birmingham, and several magazine and newspaper articles on art and local history.

The starting point for this present book was my father telling me the tale of the escaped lion at the Aston Onion Fair, which led to other stories of 'life up the terrace', and a few scribbled notes and old postcards started to get out of hand and gradually turned into the book you are now reading.

Ronald K. Moore B.A. (Hons.)

'Up the terrace' near Aston Cross with the wash house on the right and something of a luxury for a terrace, a garden

A backyard, just off Aston Road North in 1960

CHAPTER I

Daily Life and
Some Local Characters

I<small>T IS A TYPICAL SUNNY</small> Sunday morning in Aston in those squalid, hard days before the Great War. Up a typical terrace, women are sitting on stone, scrubbed front steps shelling peas into their aprons. Rather ragged lace curtains are ballooning into the street and a little gang of even more ragged children are kicking a tin-can up an entry in the next terrace. From doorways, the smell of cabbage cooking on black gas stoves drifts from dark interiors.

Most little houses in Aston and Lozells were one up and one down with a back attic and this was the scene of our homelife: a typical terrace built at right angles to the street consisting of ten small houses, five on either side of a path. In front of each was a small square yard which was elevated to the status of garden if there were a few old sinks and buckets scattered around usually containing clumps of thrift struggling for life.

The communal tap — no-one had water in the house, except when it dribbled down the walls — was flanked by a 'brewus or brewhouse, two lavatories and a 'miskin', a small rubbish and ash depository made of brick with half doors, the top for dumping and the bottom one for emptying. This was done by dustmen in greasy leather hats who loaded it into round zinc baths, cheerfully scattering ash onto the washing flapping in the yard, and struggled back up the path to the waiting horse and cart in the street.

The brewus was a small wedge-shaped building used for washing clothes, the baby and boiling the Christmas pudding. Early on winter Monday mornings, with the sky still leaden and a bitterly cold wind blowing up the yard, the women along the terrace would be up competing for first go in 'the copper', red armed and complaining and laden with armsful of washing in creaking wicker baskets. 'The copper' was the centrepiece of the brewus,

Aston Road in 1961 near the New John Street Junction. The side road is still cobbled even at this date. All has now disappeared under the Aston Expressway

A yard off Aston Road in 1961 near Aston Cross

a metal bowl sunk into a brick furnace heated by a slack or coal fire with a flue above it. A great barrel was kept inside the brewus — the tub — and once the fire was roaring up the little chimney and the water in the copper bubbling the tub was sprinkled with Hudson's Dry Powder or Rinso and the women would ladle the scalding hot water into the tub while we children of the terrace continued to stoke up the fire. Once the clothes had soaked for a while the 'Dolly Maid' came into action. Held with both hands, the stout wooden maid, looking rather like a cow's udder on a stick, was used to pummel the wet clothes in the tub in an up and down motion, loosening the dirt and setting up a deep thumping rhythm that varied with each user. Even through the steam billowing out of the doorway it was often possible to tell who was working in the tub. Then, the sodden washing had to be heaved out with the 'copper stick' transferred to bowls and put through the mangle, whose great iron handle was turned as if winding a windlass to squeeze the water out between fat wooden rollers.

By the time the first users of the brewus had finished and cleaned out the tub for the next one there was usually some activity up and down the terrace, early morning pipe smoke drifting across the yard and the hiss of bacon frying — if times were not too hard, that is. There was also a small lake in the middle of the yard by now, since the drain in the centre generally became blocked, especially on rainy days when the leaky gutters splashed water on to the yard which gushed down towards the drain and formed a pool. This would increase at an alarming rate until our Dad, cursing under his breath, would take his shoes and socks off and with trousers rolled up, giving him something of a nautical flavour, paddle through the freezing water and poke the drain violently with a stick. Rain often provided a form of entertainment. Whenever we had a downpour in the street the water would rush in a torrent along the gutter and it was quite common to see clusters of children and adults standing in doorways, watching it. Every brewhouse in the district had its tub and their constant repair kept at least one man in work. "Any tubs to mend" was a common cry throughout Lozells and Aston as he clanked his way up and down the streets replacing the iron hoops on the barrels.

The communal lavatories of our terrace — two on either side — were slotted in between the two brewhouses. Built of brick with a wooden door, these varied considerably from dismal, crumbling little huts to little homes from home with gleaming white-washed walls, raddled floors and wooden seats scrubbed snow-white. One old lady in the next terrace had even hung up a text 'The Lord is with you' — a source of some concern for little children.

Lozells Street Hall photographed by Percy Adams c.1910

Between the wars, the hall was a mecca for men of all ages, on Sunday afternoons especially, when in best Non-Conformist tradition hundreds of them met for prayers and a service. The class was noted for its fine orchestra. One of the players was a cellist by the name of Stafford Keatley, an endearing character, devout Christian and in the 30's he would have been forty years old or so. Always dressed in a crumpled grey suit and cap he was rarely seen outdoors without his beloved 'cello under his arm. He lived, as a bachelor, in Finch Road, Lozells where he used his garage as a workshop turning out badges of all kinds with the help of four or five young girl employees. There was a tennis court in his garden but he had put it to a different use. He had built a scaled down brick and stone model church with all the usual features, a few pews and hassocks, a lectern and a small harmonium. It held a dozen people and he held a service every Sunday night for staff and friends. A remarkable man in many ways. The guiding light at the hall was Mr H.S. Yoxall, a professional man in Birmingham and a J.P. He lived in one of the larger houses in Birchfield Road Handsworth, just below Haughton Road. The Sunday School was run by a Mr and Mrs Williams for many years between the wars. Next door to the hall was Mrs Jane Richardson's shop around the time of the First World War and into the twenties. The advertisements include R. Whites Kaola, Milkmaid milk, and Lyon's tea. The poster outside informs us that future speakers at the hall were to be Rev. Thomas Ewbank and Benjamin Lowe. Note the children in their Sunday best with white collars and bows in their hair.

Most lavatory pans were great unwieldy buckets and were emptied quietly at night when doors and windows were more likely to be shut tight. Up our terrace, small timid children had to face a daily terror in the little hut since the bucket had no bottom and there was a direct drop below into what might be called the River Styx. This was a running sewer almost certainly the Hockley Brook winding its way to Nechells from the Hockley valley. At best it made a vile gurgling, rumbling sound but when in full spate, as it frequently was, the echoing roar below was unnerving even for adults and imagination ran riot at the thought of the dire consquences should the building collapse while occupied. We children hated it and favoured the potty any night rather than the dash up the freezing yard followed by that dreadful gurgling.

There is no record of children disappearing into the abyss but the Brook did claim two lives on August 12 1920 when on one of its frequent overflows in Villa Street, Hockley, the water rose so quickly that two children were swept away when a wall collapsed. The awful smell and problems of clearing up after floods left little doubt that the Brook doubled as a sewer and residents of the area became so self conscious about living there that they would, in conversation, invent another area of residence. It may have been a brook but it was certainly not a babbling one.

On the lighter side, the illumination of the terrace houses was provided by gas mantle, a stubby shaped cone of gossamer like incandescent substance, so fragile that the touch of a finger would crumble it. Sealed at its top the open bottom end made of pipeclay flanges, it was fixed over the gas flow which was then lit with a match. The gas was controlled by a tap or chains which were pulled down to light or douse.

Some houses did not even have gas but were lit by a bulbous brass paraffin lamp whose wick needed constant adjusting to prevent it smoking. Upstairs we all used candles in company with the marble-topped wash stand, jug and basin and chamber pot.

Hanging in every back yard was the family zinc bath, either oval or slipper shaped and on bath nights the filling of them was a lengthy process. First kettles and pots were filled with water from the tap at the top of the terrace and then they were placed on the range fire one at a time in the one downstairs room. The old range was found in every house and each morning would find our mother, and everyone elses up the terrace kneeling down in front of it beseeching, coaxing and cursing the fire into action. As one pot became hot it was moved on to the hob on either side of the fire to simmer until all the pots were ready, and then, the bath having been placed near the hearth, all the water was tipped in. There was then another procession by members of the family to the tap up the yard to collect cold water to add to the hot. This ritual completed there was the question of who was to be first in. When small lads, we two boys would bathe at the same time so we could watch each others expressions stooping lower and lower

Lodge Road, Hockley, circa 1910

Lozells Road looking towards Villa Cross with Gower Street Boys' School on the left, on the corner of Guildford Street, Chain Walk on the right with W. Taylor's furniture shop on the corner and St. Paul's church is further down the road on the right

14

until the hot water, meeting our little bottoms, would make us straighten up smartly yelling out "too hot, too hot". Mother would then add more cold water or pick up the hand bellows and pump cold air on the surface. Next was a good soaping all over with 'Lifeboy' or yellow 'Sunlight' soap that never failed to smart our eyes, then a rinse with the flannel before being lifted out to stand in front of the fire and be rubbed down. A clean shirt was then put on for the weekend and it had to last the week at school until the following Friday.

It was easy to slop water in the hearth and dragging a full bath across the room to the door to empty in the yard was more inconvenient than pulling a plug in the stark new bathrooms which began to appear a few years later, but on cold winter nights, as gas light shone on brown linoleum, the Friday night bath in front of a crackling fire, followed by buttered toast and cocoa, was a homely affair whose passing, many years later, we looked upon with some regret and a sense of nostalgia.

While nearly everyone was poor, even long before the General Strike most folks shared food and clothes when necessary and children, on the whole, were happy. All the domestic chores were done by our mother of course, and the only help a mother was likely to have was an older daughter's while the only person she had to turn to in times of trouble was 'the woman down the street'. That was the way it was. Iron grates with their handy little side boilers were black-leaded, tables were scrubbed and front steps and frontages were swilled with water at least once a week.

Before the 1920's, when tarmacing became more popular on roads, horses and carts caused a great deal of dust and mess, grinding up and down the streets. The horse muck was a real nuisance and always managed to get splashed over the step and anyone who did not keep their bit of pavement clean was reckoned to be a bit of a trollop.

Some folks of course were poorer than others but we did not think of ourselves as poor then. Didn't everyone have bread and scrape for dinner and a 'piece' (of bread and marg.) for tea with possibly a bag of chips and some free batter from the chip shop. Lots of mothers of only thirty, up and down the street seemed to spend a lot of their time harassed, bedraggled and beslippered, yelling at the kids or were too pinched and tired to bother and stood about gossiping to neighbours up yards. A stroll along Guildford Street most days past any of the terraces would reveal clusters of women in carpet slippers and head scarves, our mother amongst them, all with arms folded, nodding sympathetically as they heard the details of the latest

The Old Oak Trees in Aston Park

Aston Church from The Park

gynaecological catastrophe. Most of these conversations over fences seemed to us to be concerned with illness and we might pretend to be occupied with a fag-packet boat in a nearby puddle while they murmured about Mrs. So and So up the street. " 'Ad it all taken away she 'as", nod nod, "cut from 'ere to there she was" more nods. "The quack says . . ." then the murmur would sink below an audible level as they reached the most interesting part and we would be left in the dark. We would, however, look on Mrs. So and So with new respect, visualizing this huge gash under her apron. Illness seemed more common then, especially in the very poor families where T.B. often existed. Everyone was more resigned to disease and death, probably due to the recent losses in the war. "Poor old bugger, gone at last, couldn't do nothing for 'im" was a very prevalent attitude.

It was the older women of the street who acted as guardians of behaviour and morals and these little groups, gossiping over garden fences, considered most people at some time or another and everyone's position and standing in the street was duly determined. This question of standing and respectability was an urgent preoccupation with many mothers. It was easier for the men; at weekends they could change their 10/- 'light boots' for polished boots, tradesmen could wear stiff collars and bowlers could be donned by anyone with pretensions to 'respectability'. (Working men always wore caps of course.)

Standing was partially determined by house rents — 2/6 a week for a back-to-back in Ventnor Terrace and 4/6 for a 'two up two down' in Guildford Street. It was difficult to 'put on airs' as Mother said, up the terrace, but some girls had music lessons, their mothers hoping that they would 'get on' and lots of mothers in Bright Terrace, Ventnor Terrace and along Guildford Street went to enormous lengths — doing the traditional 'scrimping and saving' and going without so that their children would be well turned out for school. Income had little to do with respectability. One could be 'trade' with aspirations or an unskilled workman, it was up to the mother to bring up the children properly, whether Dad spent half his time lounging on the kitchen chair or not.

Most people 'knew their place, and stuck to saving up for something prestigious, that preferably could be put in the window, to help their standing. A few people up the street, particularly tradesmen, but some working families too, clearly had thoughts of mixing with middle class Handsworth, but since men like our Dad earned around £80 a year and an office worker living in Hamstead Road earned four times that amount there

Aston Villa Wesleyan Chapel at the end of George Street, Lozells, looking towards Lozells Road at the Villa Cross end. On the right in the Lozells Road is Sid Amey's pub, then William Wicks' sweets and tobacco shop with the Wills Gold Flake sign outside. Next door is Thomas Sinisters shoe shop, proclaiming above the door that he only uses best English leather, then came Mr Johnston and Mr Dares electrical business

was little chance of Lozells families moving into the heady atmosphere of Handsworth.

My own first awareness of life came at the age of three — in 1912 — when I was in hospital with the common illness known as 'the fever'. This was, of course, scarlet fever and the black, van-type ambulances of the day were a frequent sight on their way to and from hospital.

The hospital where I was confined was at Little Bromwich and when recalling the ward, I see a dark-haired nurse standing by a heating stove with a white enamel mug of tea, which she was slowly sipping, in her hand. For years afterwards, the sight of a white enamel mug brought that scene to mind. It had a special smell connected with it, not easily described, but redolent of sweetness and warmth.

1916 was memorable for another episode in my young life. It brought my first introduction to sorrow and grief. My best friend and first little pal was Billy Tovey who lived at the top house on our side of the terrace. He was an only child, delicate in physique, quiet and shy and two years older than I. I remember him as I last saw him, sixty seven years ago, dressed in a navy blue jacket, knee breeches of the same colour, a white Eton collar and wearing a cap. We had been playing in the street one day when he complained of difficulty in breathing. He went into his house and I never saw him again. Within two days he had died from T.B., a dread killer then known as consumption. The news of his death was kept from me until just before his funeral when I sat with my mother behind the lace curtain at our one downstairs window. Bearers carried Billy in his coffin down the terrace and I burst into a deep sobbing and buried my head in my mother's arms. I never really understood the references to death made by adults during the war but now realized that a person was never to be seen again and I wept for my first friend Bill whom I have never forgotten.

Funerals tended to be more ornate than today, not up the terraces of course but in the better areas of Aston and Handsworth especially. Some times we would see a pair of jet black horses with plumes pulling a hearse up Aston High Street. Everyone wore black and the widow continued to wear her 'weeds' for at least a month before showing her face in the street. When a baby died, the coffin was usually carried by four girls wearing white dresses and their heads covered with a white veil.

While poverty contributed to many illnesses and caused much hardship it also initiated some ingenious moneysaving ideas. A popular source of income for we children was collecting the manure conveniently left up the street by the many delivery horses. We shovelled the steaming muck into home-made barrows or buckets and sold it for ½d. or 1d. to anyone who had a little garden. If childhood is at least partly measured in smells which cause instant recall when encountered again many years later, then fresh horse muck up the Lozells Road must be near the top of the list of evocative smells. In the same way, the sweet, cool smell of fresh ice-cream brings to mind the Italian woman who sold ice-cream in little egg-shaped wafers on

Ken Moore (authors father) outside number 5 Park Lane, Aston

Furnace Lane, which was a narrow alley running from the Gower Street/Guildford Street junction down through Gerrard Street and Clifford Street to Porchester Street

Sunday afternoons, from a small hardcart, similar to those used by the winkle seller and the knife grinder. She often stood outside an outdoor, where children were regular visitors, collecting bottles of 'Loose beer' (with sticky paper seals over the stopper when sold to youngsters) for Dad.

Back at home, in the winter especially, our Mother used to get out the rag rug in the evenings. For many months this was an old sack with bits of coloured cloth tied at one end in rows. She used to get old jerseys, curtains and frocks from the jumble sales at the Salvation Army in Nursery Road or from the rag barrows in the Bull Ring and she showed us how to cut them into strips and push them through the holes in the canvas with a little wooden-handled tool. She would sit for hours in front of the range with the sack on her lap, surrounded by heaps of cut rags with we three children squatting on the old rag rug, jostling to be nearest the grate. The old rug was, by now, flat and colourless from constant trampling. Mother would work on one end and we on the other. When complete, the rugs were a blaze of colour and very cosy to sit on, the alternative being the cold lino, so we were all keen to see the new rug finished. In time, it too would go dull and flat and off we started all over again.

The little fire used to roar up the chimney once it was stoked up and the whole range became piping hot. To save on the coal the next day, we generally made use of the heat by cooking something for tomorrow's dinner so a small steam pudding might be simmering and bubbling in the stewing pot hanging off the iron rod that swung over the fire. When the hob was really glowing, the cat, who tended to live dangerously and often slept in the oven on an old jersey would have to vacate his bed with a yowl and leap out looking accusingly at everyone.

While kids along the street were shovelling manure into buckets for a few pence, some of their Dads did a nice little business as back street bookmakers. This was all quite illegal of course, so bets had to be well hidden should the local copper on the beat be suspicious. One man in the next terrace — a mangle repairer — hid his book in the dog's kennel and it took a brave policeman to grope about amongst Fido's old bones.

Another handy way of earning a few shillings was by selling 'El Dorado' ice cream from a box on a tricycle gaily marked 'stop me and buy one'. A Mr. Dix, who lived in Finch Road, used to regularly ply to and fro on summer evenings with his box of slowly melting ice cream. He could be seen sometimes with an old car tyre on his back — picked up on his rounds — and he used these to sole and heel childrens' shoes. The shoes tended to

Brougham Street Lozells, running between Nursery Road and Will's Street on a sunny morning in the early 1930's. There are four cars and lorries visible but no horses. At number 16 was The Bath Tavern and along the street were a number of small 'back garden shed' industries including a pencil maker, a ham boiler, a drawing pin maker and a boot maker

Clifford Street Lozells at the Wheeler Street junction c.1908. On the right corner is The Daisy Ale Stores and The Crown Stores is on the left

Aston.   *Six Ways.*

Note: The office & the boy 11 - 11 on day Nov 9:8

Aston, Six Ways. A Wrench Series post card taken c. 1901 three years before the tramway was built in 1904, with Birchfield Road on the left and Witton Road on the right. Behind the corner of the Christ Church Baptist Chapel on the right of the picture is the Avery Scales Receiving depot in Witton Road. By the mid-twenties, Harry Turnhill the butcher had his shop there. Next door is John Atkinson the chemist who was still there in 1926, then came a wine shop run by George Earles and Dr Norris at number 3. On the left of the picture is Six Ways post office and telegraph office run by Florence Tart in the 20's

leave strange tracks in the snow but when it was wet, the Dix kids did not have to walk on their heels through puddles which was more than could be said for most of us up the terrace.

The Rudds, Mr and Mrs were an enterprising couple down the Lozells Road in Guildford Street. They had a long yard packed with live fowl and rabbits which were replenished daily. They made a living by selling these and the yard was also the slaughter-house so that chickens still enjoying a limited existance in the yard had plenty of opportunity to see what happened to their mates. Mr Rudd, a short, stout man with a bald, pink head and a few straggling white hairs always contrived to have a growth of stubble on his pink cheeks; never a beard, just a disinclination to shave more than once a week. He would sit on a box in the yard, immersed in a cloud of feathers plucking away at a little pile of hot carcases. Then when he and everything else was covered in down he would start on the rabbits and before long there would be a row of soggy little pelts drying on the yard wall.

23

LOZELLS STREET HALL A.C. TEAM, 1906,

PHOTO. H. WARWICK.

Winners of the Birmingham and District A.G.A. Senior Shield and Barnes' Cup.

The Lozells Street Hall athletics team in 1906 after they had won the Barnes Cup and the Birmingham and District A.G.A. Senior Shield

REV. W L. WATKINSON.

A RESPECTFUL REMINDER TO YOU.

WEDNESDAY, JUNE 23RD, 1909.

Opening of New Lecture Hall

AT THE

LOZELLS ST. WESLEYAN MISSION,
ASTON MANOR.

3-15 p.m.   RECEPTION and OPENING by
MRS. A. WALTER LOWE.

3-30 p.m.   SERMON by
REV. W. L. WATKINSON.

8-0 p.m.   An ADDRESS by
REV. W. L. WATKINSON.

CHAIRMAN :—E. J. HUNT, ESQ., J.P. C.C.

WILL YOU PLEASE TRY AND ATTEND?
DO! DO!! DO!!!

An announcement of the opening of the new lecture hall at Lozells Street Hall, in 1909

Mrs Rudd looked like a little mother hen herself. Brown beady eyes always switching from side to side, a twitching of the neck in a to and fro motion and both arms hidden under a shawl gave the impression that she might cluck at any moment. The smell from their yard was to be avoided and many people would cross the street earlier than was necessary to avoid it. You could always tell if someone had visited the Rudds. They tended to have a white haze about them.

Then there was Joe Bryant, our lamplighter. A tallish man, he was a well-known figure before the Great War with his lamplighting rod resting on his right shoulder and a pickled cabbage birthmark covering the whole of his face. He attended to his lamps at a fast pace, lighting or dousing them and in the early morning he combined the job with that of 'knocker up' for anyone who had to be up early for work. Then, his sharp tap at an upstairs window with the rod would be answered by the flaring up of the gas mantle lit in the bedroom as acknowledgement. He cleaned the lamp glass too during the day when he would dispense with his rod and carry a ladder on his shoulder. A most meticulous man, even-tempered in spite of his disfigurement, he liked his drink but never during working hours. An Irish gentleman.

Pawnshops were an integral part of the daily life and hard times and Laura Lyons, who lived in Guildford Street around the First World War recalled their own family's poverty well. ''I went to the bits of outings and parties given by the police — the home-made cakes and bread-puddings. I use to go to the pawn shop for my Mother with the washing after Mother wash it on Mondays. I use to hate it. What about the 'Blood Tub Matinees', 1d. and ½d. ice-cream pie and the pigeon flyers on Sunday afternoons! They use to finish up fighting over the races and down would come the black police vans to get them in and the copper whistle going.

I had some happy times. My brothers and me use to go to free breakfasts — bread and jam and cocoa and Mother use to get free dinners because she was breast feeding and she use to save me her pudding and bring it out. We was very poor. My Dad worked on the salvage — a dustman for 2s 10d a week. Half bread puddings in paper from the coffee shop by us. Remember the cow heels and tripe and pigs' feet and trotters? Oh, I could go on! You wouldn't have it like I had to live with!''

There were around 30 pawnbrokers in Aston and Lozells during the mid 1920's and many even had other pawnshops elsewhere in the city. They were

The old Aston Cross
c.1885

often run by one lady like Amelia Creswick's shop in Church Lane, Aston, and Sarah Moore's in Clifford Street, Lozells.

Monday mornings generally saw a good queue outside the pawnshops. As kids we sometimes found ourselves on cold drizzly Monday mornings joining the line outside one shop or another clutching a pathetic bundle of freshly-washed sheets, Dad's best, and only suit or whatever else looked faintly respectable. When our turn came, the owner would feel the clothes disparagingly between thumb and fore-finger, shake his head and mutter about no call for this sort of thing, poor stuff, and offer a pittance for our best linen. Then off we would go, coppers chinking in hand and pawn ticket safely tucked away so that we could, hopefully, redeem our 'poor stuff' on Friday when our Dad was paid. Our first stop was usually White's or Rowbotham's, the butchers on Lozells Road, for a nice 6d. lamb chop. That was if we had done well at the pawnshop. If we had not, then we might have a piece cut from the great white folds of tripe on marble slabs in the window or two anaemic looking boiled pigs' trotters to go with the pot of peas that Mother would have simmering and popping on the gas ring at home.

Mr James' pawn shop was on the corner of Clifford Street and Wheeler Street. A double-fronted shop, it was presided over by the white-haired, retired J.P. who seemed rather stern to we children but was quite approachable and if the queue was too long outside Sarah Moore's we would go to his shop.

Some women would refuse to rely on the pawnshop, however desperate things became while others organized their housekeeping on 'the Monday bundle'. Bundles were usually retrieved the following Saturday for 'a penny in the shilling.' Our Father was generally in work, as a skilled machine operator in various local factories, and Mother rarely had to hock anything. If she did so, then it was a spare sheet or odd shirt that went. Once however, without our Dad's knowledge, she hocked his best suit and on finding out he was so wild that he threw a cabbage at her. The cabbage was alright but

The new clock tower at Aston Cross in 1905 with Park Road on the left and Lichfield Road on the right

Mother had to go to Dudley Road Hospital with a badly bruised eye. Dad was sorry afterwards but he was probably more angry at the idea of being seen to be 'in distress' than at the temporary loss of his best suit. Such was the importance of 'family image' in those days. No use having an aspidistra and net curtains if 'the missis' is seen up the pawnshop etc.

Lichfield Road Aston. Grosvenor Road is on the left and Holborn Hill and Thimble-Mill Lane on the right under the railway bridge with the Swanpool Tavern, run by Frank Rufford in the twenties, on the corner. Next to the Swanpool the awning of Albert Shaw's china and glass shop can just be made out and on this side of Holborn Hill is Mrs Katherine Jones' dining room on the corner, then Mrs Hall's sweet shop, Matthew's chip shop and the Brittania Public House with its two big gas lamps outside. The landlord was George Wilkinson. With the apple and orange boxes outside in the foreground is Walt Stafford's greengrocery shop. On the left, on the corner of Grosvenor Road, Frank Fellow's clothes shop can be seen with a sheet keeping the sun from his garments then came a cramped row of little shops including, next door Sid Matthews the butcher, Bill Gibberson the tobacconist and Mrs Dewick's sweet shop. Next to the bridge is the entrance to the station. Mr Albert Chamberlain was station-master in the mid twenties. In the distance is an early tramcar, one of the first batch of 21 to appear in Birmingham.

CHAPTER II

Pastimes and Entertainments

A<small>FTER THE GREAT WAR</small>, there seemed to be a sudden increase in street entertainers in Aston and Lozells. Many were ex-servicemen, crippled and out of work. Some were competent musicians and drew a good crowd although mostly of ragged children while others seemed to possess little of no gift for their particular choice of instrument. Most contrived to look suitably derelict and pathetic and were often amputees, which tended not to help the standard of musicianship. The majority of families could barely keep themselves in food and clothes and had little to spare for one man bands and the like, however decrepit a picture they made. Most of them must have made some sort of a living because whenever we saw any of these grey-faced medal-festooned old soldiers clashing, rattling and thumping his way into a coffee shop they appeared to be weighed down with coppers, bulging in greatcoat pockets.

As for we children, we were more than pleased if we could scrape three pence together for a big bag of perriwinkles between us from the perriwinkle-man's handcart on a Sunday afternoon. Then we spent hours picking the winkles out of their shells with pins.

One well-known street singer is said to have died a rich woman, although she feigned poverty of course. Her 'patch' on pre-war Sundays was the Six Ways area. A small bonneted and shawled old woman, with an intimidating manner and limited repertoire, she sang 'Count your blessings count them one by one and it will surprise you what the Lord has done'. This was repeated relentlessly up and down the streets and along terraces and back again so that her shrill, wailing tones could be heard becoming stronger, fading away and then strengthening again as she plied to and fro. The phrase was frequently broken by "thank you very much", especially on Sundays when many of us would be trotting along to Sunday school and rather than pass her by and arouse her venom we would donate our 'missionary money'. She cursed anyone who was reluctant to 'give freely'

The Aston Silver Band who won the Brierley Hill Band Contest in 1901, the Water Orton Contest in 1904 the Northfield Champion Challenge Cup and cornet and euphonium medals in 1906

The Birmingham City Police Band of 1924

and sometimes cursed them — fluently — even when they did, just for good measure. "Blasted bit" she would snarl, then continue with 'Count your blessings'. We always tried to hide up a terrace when we heard her coming rather than face her.

One of the greatest musical attractions in the street was the barrel organ. Most looked like a keyless piano on two wheels and pushed within two shafts by 'the organ grinder' they produced, via a perforated paper roll engaging on set, tuned pegs, the songs of the day by the turning of a handle. One old man, in a ragged army greatcoat, had a little barrel organ on a thick leather strap over his shoulder. It worked in the same way as the bigger ones but made a thinner tinkling sound and the weight of it had made him so bent that he had to peer under his cap to see where he was going.

Some organs had a small monkey, usually with a tiny red fez on it's head tethered to the organ by a long chain which enabled it to scamper among the onlookers with a collecting bowl.

Some times people jigged about to the music and women could be seen prancing up and down, cackling uncontrollably, kicking fat 'corned beef' legs in the air — legs pale and blotchy from sitting too close to the fire.

For many people, the hurdy-gurdy was the only excuse for a 'knees-up'. Sometimes, someone up a terrace might have a piano, always out of tune, and on warm summer evenings it would be dragged out into the yard for a sing-song. Then all the terrace would turn out, the kids would be sent to the Weymouth Arms for a few bottles of beer and folks from nearby yards would lean over the fence and join in.

We often wondered, as kids, how the hurdy-gurdy men made a living, since few people gave anything in the street then one of the regulars, a pale wizened but cheery old chap, told me that 9/10ths of his money was made in coffee shops and the cheaper public houses. He would jangle out a few tunes then go in with a collecting cup. Then he would play one more tune for the sake of pride. He was a performer, not just being paid to go away you see. Some organ grinders had a mate who would do the rounds for them, 'catch the drop' he called it, but few could afford this. The barrel organ cost 30/- a week to hire, in the 1930's, and the week's takings were only likely to be around £2.

On Sunday mornings, the Birmingham Police Band used to play in Elkinton Street Park, which was called a park but was all concrete, the band-stand being the only thing in it. During the sunny silence of the hot

The Holte Almshouses in Aston Lane c. 1926

summer days, I would sit on my Grandma's front step in Elkinton Street *Daily Mail* boots off, feeling the baking pavement through my socks, with 'taters' at both ends, listening to the marches floating down the street. We often visited Gran on Sundays and Elkinton Street became a sort of second home and while it was just outside the boundary, everyone thought of themselves as living in Aston.

Sunday was about the only time when it seemed peaceful up Elkinton Street. During the week we could hear the trams lumbering and grinding along Newtown Row and Aston Road North and there was always the sound of iron rims on the cobbles as delivery carts trundled up and down the streets.

As carts passed by we lads could often be seen clinging to their back, for the ride, until someone in the street would shout "Oi put yer whip be'ind". This would tell the driver that he had passengers and he would crack his whip over his shoulder to shift them. Many was the time that we dropped off into a pile of horse-muck — not difficult to do since there was so much about in those days. Dad reckoned that each horse dropped around twenty pounds of manure a day. We reckoned that with the thousands of horses in Brum it was a wonder we were not buried in the stuff.

Delivery horses were often seen dragging along huge carts full of coal or scrap iron — loads that really needed a pair of horses and on wet days especially, they would sometimes slip on the cobbles going uphill and fall down with a clatter of hooves and a sickening thud. They always looked pathetic but seldom seemed really hurt. They usually refused to get up for some time, despite passers by heaving on the harness, as if to say "I'm just having a rest before I continue pulling this ruddy lot". The horses we most liked were the perchorons and shires with flowing manes and great fetlocks. They were used in pairs by the breweries to pull the heavy drays and were generally turned out beautifully, with gleaming brasses and beribboned tails.

When we were very young, the number 5 trams clanking along the Lozells Road were still fairly new, having only changed from steam to electric

The Salvation Army Hall in Nursery Road, between Villa Street and Church Street. In the middle of the last century, No 5 Nursery Terrace, as it was then known, was for three years the home of the Rev. George Browne and his family. His daughters all achieved remarkable married status, although he was a little known Wesleyan minister himself. Louisa was the mother of Stanley Baldwin, the prime minister, Alice, the eldest, was the mother of Rudyard Kipling, and Georgina married the painter Sir Edward Burne-Jones. The fourth daughter, Agnes, married Sir Edward Poynter, first Slade Professor of fine art at University College London.

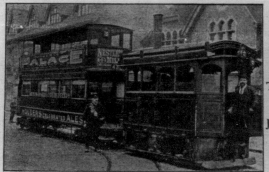

In Remembrance of
SALTLEY, PERRY BARR, WITTON, & LOZELLS OLD STEAM TRAMS

WHICH STARTED
SERVICE
NOVEMBER 25th,
1884.

PASSING AWAY
OWING
TO AN ELECTRIC
SHOCK
JANUARY 1st, 1907.

" Let not ambition mock their useful toils,
Their homely joys and destiny obscure."

[Photo by]   [P. King.

An 'In Memorium' card for steam trams. The tramway was built in 1884 in the Lozells area
and electric trams took over in 1907

Tramcar 714 about to turn right from Victoria Road into Park Road on its way to the depot at
Witton. The date is the early 1940's and the roads are still cobbled. The tram was built by the
Brush Falcon Works at Loughborough in 1925 and was withdrawn in 1953. The advertisements
include Star Cigarettes and Digger Tobacco at 9d. an ounce.

34

traction in 1906 and their lights seemed very exciting at night. In the late 20's and 30's they were outshone by the bright street lamps but when we could afford the fare, 1½d, we loved to catch a tram down the Lichfield Road, muffled against the east wind sitting upstairs. The seats were a little like garden seats, hard wooden slats and none too comfortable for any distance, but since few people could afford the fare for more than a few stops, it did not matter very much. We liked the sounds; the whining noise as the yellow and black front appeared in the distance, the sound of our boots on the metal stairs as we clattered 'on top', then two clear pings on the bell and the whining clanking started again, building up to a crescendo as we swayed and rattled down the hill towards Aston Station. If we closed our eyes all the racket gave the impression of great speed, and upstairs, we had the blue flashes from the trolley head as well. Sweeping under Aston bridge, everyone would duck involuntarily because the bridge was so low that the overhead wires dipped down to the edge of the road and the trolley head dropped level with the top of the car.

We used to get off by the bridge, buy a gobstopper at Mrs Dewick's sweet shop by the station entrance and walk up on to the station to poke about and talk to the station master. The station was rather like the tram, full of bells, levers and bits of polished brass and mahogony. Sometimes he used to make us some coffee, which was a bit of a treat since we only ever had tea at home. It was an odd mixture of chicory and coffee that he boiled in a beer can and sweetened with 'Goat Brand' condensed milk and sugar. The smell has long gone in the march of progress, together with soot and steam, but recollections of it bring back the rattling trams and goods trains thundering through Aston Station.

Going back up the hill on a number 78 or 79 tram, sometimes in the winter the conductor had to ask people by the door to stand up so that he could get at the box of sand under their seats and throw some on the line when the wheels were slipping. Tram mishaps of various sorts were common in those days. We were once rattling down the hill in Aston Road when the trolley started to whip from side to side as the tram pitched. The overhead wire must have been slack for next, the head jumped off and we ground to a halt and had to wait for a repair gang to arrive. Meanwhile, a row of tramcars had started to pile up in a queue behind and the road was soon crammed with trams full of passengers complaining and peering out of the window.

In very cold weather, an iced up track was often a problem and we sometimes saw the tramways workmen by the side of the road with roaring braziers of coal to heat pots of water which would be poured on the points

Lozells Road, taken by the photographer Percy Adams, looking towards Six Ways with Berners Street on the right and Howard Shepherds wine shop on the corner selling Bass ale from the wood and Gilbey's 'Invalid Port' for 2/6 a bottle. Next door is Harry Fitters watch and clock shop then Clara and Florence Horsley who were milliners. Over the road on the edge of the picture is Robert Dale's hosiery and clothes business, Arthur Wharam's umbrella shop and Yapp's the drapers on the corner of Hartington Road. On the other side with the delivery cart outside is William Bowkett's fish and chip shop and Henry Playfair's shoe shop.

Hidden in the photographic mist is Wilton Street on the left and right and on the right hand junction stood the Lozells Picture House, doomed to be destroyed by bombs in 1941 when the manager was killed. Still in the mist forty yards further along Lozells Road was the site of the 'Old Skating Rink' Picture House, a low corrugated iron building, closed during the first war. Just beyond and over the road was James Street with its steep hill. A large part of this suffered **great damage and loss of life by aerial mines in the same raid which struck the Lozells Picture** House. Across Lozells Road was Wheeler Street with its tramway to town. Just inside still stands what was Lozells Congregational Church and is now a Sikh Temple. Back on to Lozells Road stands St. Paul's Anglican church, now owned by the First Assembly Church of God (West Indian) The tram would have been a number 5 and since there is not a car to be seen and dresses are still long, the date is probably c. 1910. Next door to St. Paul's was Gower Street Junior School, now an empty space, and the police station next door currently serves as a department of Social Welfare. Across the road on the corner of Guildford Street is Chain Walk so called because in Queen Victoria's reign there were trees lining the road linked by ornamental iron chains. The last road on the right was William Street then Six Ways opened out.

36

to stop them freezing up. Snow rarely stopped a Birmingham tram as they were especially fitted with wooden snowploughs at the first sign of a fall, but on inclines like Lichfield Road the driver often had to have two or three runs at the slope to break up the ice on the track. It the worst came to the worst and a tram did become stuck then another one would come up behind and shunt it along until the hill was safely negotiated.

There were not many serious tram accidents but Dad recalled one in nearby Hockley in the early days of electrification when, October 1907, a tram had run away down the hill in Lodge Road. It had stopped at the clock in Warstone Lane where the driver had told the inspector he thought the brakes were faulty. The inspector dismissed the idea, hopped on board and set off himself only to find the brakes had totally gone. As the tram charged down the hill, gathering speed, the terrified top-deck passengers started to leap off in panic and a number were killed before the tram eventually crashed lower down the hill. There were few accidents as dramatic as this but a number of trams turned over when taking a bend too fast and as motor cars became more popular we saw a few collisions, particularly at the Lozells and Wheeler Street junction.

When we were young, we used to look on the gypsies' visits as a bit of an entertainment, more through our mother's gullible attitude to them than anything else. By the time we children were grown up, the end drawer of the back kitchen table was crammed full with pegs. Mother thought it was unlucky not to buy from the gypsies so she always did, whether we needed any pegs or not. The pegs were made from a thick twig, about ¾ inch, split into two and bound together with a cut piece of old tin can.

In addition to the street musicians and others trying to make a living on the pavements there were plenty of beggars who made no pretence of selling anything or entertaining but stood around in all weathers holding out a cap. We lads always noticed one especially, since he appeared to have no legs and propelled himself along on a board with wheels—much like our go-carts made from old prams. He was quite expert at steering through the crowds along the Lozells Road and we reckoned that he would have beaten us in a race.

Despite the general poverty, pubs still did a roaring trade and it was common to see a wife, children clutching her skirt, attempting to get her husband out of the pub before all the housekeeping was spent. Every weekend the Temperance Society, Band of Hope and Salvation Army had a field day extolling the evils of strong drink.

High Street Aston with the Barton's arms in the early 1930's. Potter's Hill is on the right and 'The Globe Electric Palace' on the left on the corner of New Street. The Globe was opened in 1913 and closed in 1955

POST CARD

FOR COMMUNICATION ADDRESS

With Compliments from . .
VILLA CROSS PICTURE HOUSE.

PATRIA
THE
NEW & FASCINATING SERIAL
—— COMMENCES ON ——
XMAS EVE,
AND CONTINUES EVERY
Monday, Tuesday & Wednesday
FOR 15 WEEKS.

Pathe Freres Cinema Ltd Series Copyright
PRINTED IN ENGLAND

An advertisement for The Villa Cross Picture House in Heathfield Road Handsworth which opened in 1912. The facade has a large round arch, rather like the Victoria Playhouse Aston, and a circular window. The inside is vaulted with lavishly decorated walls embossed with plaster cupids, swags, angels and floral designs.

In 1919 the population of the terrace increased by one male as Mrs Hindle acquired a new husband, Alf. He was a thick-set, dark-haired man in his 40's who was quickly absorbed into the life of our little community. We never knew Alf's surname and his lady-love continued to be known as Mrs Hindle. They were the only ones ever to dress in their Sunday best to walk the short distance to the Weymouth Arms on the corner. We lads were fascinated by pubs and would push open the door of the public bar and look inside curiously. There was always a powerful smell of beer and those who did not smoke tobacco chewed 'twist', a hard wad of dark brown tobacco. This being the era of spitting, there were always metal spitoons placed at strategic points around the room but since T.B. was rife there were notices on trams and elsewhere outlining the dangers of contracting the disease.

Licensing laws were very tight in those days and children were never seen in pubs though there were often a couple of little kids standing shivering outside waiting for Dad. On cold, damp nights especially when the street was plunged into darkness between the lamps, pubs like the Weymouth Arms looked very cosy to us as we passed by on our way to Mrs Swingswood's chipshop or Kench's round in Gerrard Street to collect the supper. Dancing fires in grates, mahogony bars, with brass and china handles and gleaming spitoons glimpsed through swing doors beckoned to us and we looked forward to when we too could stand at the bar with one foot on the brass rail and, caps pushed well back, order our pints of Ansell's.

The best non-free entertainment, when a few pennies were available, was found at the 'pictures'. Before the Great War, the industry was fairly new and all the films were silent but immensely popular, even when jerky and constantly breaking down—to an accompaniment of shouts and boos.

Around the time of the war, as young lads, my brother and I often went to the Lozells Picture House and sometimes The Aston Picture Palace, also in Lozells Road. These were the earliest Kinematographs in the areas. The Lozells Picture House stood opposite William Street and next to No. 5 Lozells Road, 'The Co-op'. It was a dowdy, corrugated iron building of one storey, lit by gaslight and had been converted from the old skating rink so we always knew it as 'The skating Rink'. During the war it was condemned as a fire hazard then it reopened as 'Jones and Neale, Aluminium Ware', run by Alf Homer.

A new Lozells picture house, in Lozells Road, had a skating rink attached to it and was owned by The Erdington Rink Company. It was the proud

The Theatre Royal, Aston

An advertisement for
the Hippodrome in 1904
featured on a post card

BIRMINGHAM'S FAVORITE VARIETY
THEATRE.

TWICE NIGHTLY,
6-30 and 9.

TWICE NIGHTLY,
6-30 and 9.

MATINEE EVERY THURSDAY 2-30.

possessor of one of the new Compton Organs with two manuals, played by Reginald Fort in the early days before he went on to be the B.B.C. theatre organist. This was all very new and exciting and a decided improvement on the old lady bashing away on the 'Skating Rink' picture house piano. The skating rink part of the building was festooned with flags inside, as were many rinks then, which waved about us as we tore round doing our impressive cross-over steps on the corners.

In the 20's there was the Aston Cross Picture House in Witton Road, run by Edward Couchman and William Devey and opposite the Barton's Arms, the Globe Electric Theatre with its white domed roof. This was managed by Richard Holder. Could this have been the grandson of Henry Holder whose concert hall in Coleshill Street our old grandad used to talk about? The Globe had its front entrance at the junction of High Street and New Street Aston. This was the entrance for 'better' seats, the front and rear stalls at 4d. and 6d. A few yards inside New Street was a little window set into the wall where we queued for the front stalls at 2d. a time. In the 20's, when we were short of 2d. we used to pay with a couple of jam-jars and still have a comic or some sweets 'thrown in'.

By the 1930's, all our favourite flea-pits were abandoned for the new carpeted, flamboyant super-cinemas, like 'The Orient' decorated with eastern scenes. Now, there were posh, uniformed 'commissionaires' who stood outside yelling which seats were still available. There were 'foyers' where we could study the 'coming soon' posters. There were wrapped ice-creams and something new called a choc-ice and there was warmth, comfort and privacy—important when we lads started to take an interest in girls. There was little privacy up the terrace and a luxurious seat in the back stalls was a big improvement on 'the monkey run' up by Aston church. Why this was so called, no-one knew. It was a patch of ground where boys walked in one direction and girls in the other so that on each circuit interested parties could eye each other and engage in appropriate banter.

On Saturday night, Gosta Green open market was packing away just when the pictures were opening, so sometimes we would make the walk up there to buy a 'pennorth of specks'—speckled apples going off a little, or a bag of broken biscuits for 1d. By this time I had moved from Lozells to Elkinton Street, Aston so 'The Globe' was now the 'local pictures'. Another Aston picture house was 'The Victoria Playhouse' in Victoria Road and later the 'Orient Cinema' opened in High Street Aston. It had no organ but records were played in the interval and scented disinfectant was sprayed everywhere to kill germs. Everyone hated this and it did little to perpetuate the oriental atmosphere.

Will Leslie's entertainers in Aston, c. 1910

This pre-first world war picture shows a cinema in Lozells Road, Birmingham, next door to the No.5 Co-op Branch. Kelly's Directory of 1911 describes it as Aston Picture Palace, but at other times it has had other names - and sometimes no name at all.

The Aston Picture Palace Lozells Road opened in 1910 next door to No. 5 The Co-op, and opposite William Street. All has now been obliterated in the Six-Ways 'development'. The proprietor was Fred Jeffery

42

The new 'picture palaces' were much the same everywhere. Children could lose themselves in the series and comedies. We saw the silent antics of Ford Stirling and his Keystone Cops, Buster Keaton, Chester Conklin and many others. We all particularly loved Pearl White in The Exploits of Elaine and The Perils of Pauline where she seemed to spend much of her time tied to a railway track as a train was approaching. Then 'To be continued next week' would come on and up went the lights to a chorus of 'oohs and aahs'. Some of us could not afford to go each week so we never did know what happened next.

A great hero of the boys was the cowboy star Eddie Polo, whose daredevil exploits and rescuing of maidens in distress were in the same frustrating serial form. The most successful of the Eddie Polo series was 'The Broken Coin' where the plot centred around the search for half a broken coin before the hero could thwart the villains and win the girl. For the duration of the serial the plot overflowed into the streets of Aston and boys could be seen searching enthusiastically in cracked walls for the broken coin.

Then in 1918—sensational, unbelievable! Eddie Polo was coming all the way from California to make personal appearances in British cinemas and the Lozells Picture House was one of them. We waited impatiently for the big day to arrive. It was to be a special childrens' show and as the time came a packed hall sat fidgeting expectantly. Suddenly there was a commotion at the entrance and a hundred little heads turned to see a white stetson over the partition at the small foyer. The cheering burst out as he swung into the aisle, immaculate in cowboy gear, and tried to walk down to the screen but crowds of boys gathered round him slapping him on the back. He wore a red kerchief, grey blouse, grey trousers tucked into high-heeled boots with clinking spurs and round his waist was a gun belt studded with bullets holding two pearl-handled revolvers. What a sight! When he had gone it dawned on us that we had heard him speak for the first time. An idol had come to life.

The visit of a real cowboy to Lozells injected a new life into picture-going in the area. W.S. Hart, Hoot Gibson and co., heroes all, busily chased red Indians to the frenzied accompaniment of resident pianists bashing out Suppès 'Light Cavalry'. The whoops of the pursuing posses mingled with those of the audience. The pictures had come to stay.

When we were a little older, another possibility presented itself for weekend entertainment and this was dancing. By the late twenties, Saturday evenings would find flocks of girls trotting along Witton Road and Lozells

Aston Swimming Baths in Victoria Road. In the 1920's Mr R. Hoggins was superintendant

Catherine Street Mission Cricket Club in 1912. Holding the cricket bat on the left is Albert Brown who kept a shop in Catherine Street, which ran off the east side of Lichfield Road just past Aston Cross

Road to Albert Hall in Chain Walk, Six Ways, with full length dresses tucked up in the bad weather. There were no cars and few could afford the tram fare so it was common to see girls walking.

Albert Hall was very popular, with local bands trying to imitate Ambrose, Harry Roy, Billy Merrin, Roy Fox, Ray Noble and, of course, Charlie Kunz piano playing. We called it 'Amies' but really it was 'Madam Amies Academy' and Amie herself lived next door. The hall was known as 'The Coffin' by us since that was what it looked like. The resident band was a simple affair called 'Phillips Band' and was run by Amie's son-in-law, Mr Hemmings, who played the saxaphone. It was like innumerable other small dance bands who provided jazzily, jolly music for couples sliding around the chalky floor doing the fox trot, 'one step' and unathletic version of the waltz. Any sort of extravagent activity was ruled out by lack of space and anyway, the atmosphere was rather sedate at Amies—until the jitterbug crept in during the late 30's that is.

Once we had left school, at fourteen, and were at work, we could get a bit of practice at home with our dance steps by buying the little 6 inch records from Woolworths in the Bull Ring for 6d. each. The old clumsy gramophone with horns and phonographs, like our Nans, had been replaced by smaller, portable ones. Ours was a small black one with the His Masters Voice dog on the inside of the lid. It was second hand of course, from the pawnshop and we were always running out of steel needles so we used the old ones over and over which made the records even more scratchy.

Amies lacked sophistication. There was none of the fancy decor found at 'The Palais de dance', with Bert Thomas' smartly turned out band and 'The West End' with 'Tony and The Red Aces' and two dance floors, but Amies was ours. We knew the girls who would be likely to turn up and it had a homely atmosphere, partly due to the fact that it was so packed that we could hardly move. Many of the girls we had already met on 'the monkey run'.

Various schools in the area ran 'night school dances' at this time, with an entrance fee of 6d. especially Gower Street and Albert Road and from when we were 14 years old, together with 'Amies', social life began here. The hairdresser on the corner of Rifle Crescent and Victoria Road did a roaring trade on Friday nights when girls waited their turn for a 'top wave' at 6d. a time, called Marcel waving.

Aston Swimming baths in Victoria Road was another venue, especially for we boys. There were two swimming baths at Victoria Road, first and second class, costing, in the late 1920's, 6d. and 4d. The cheaper pool had a

Aston Girl Guides c. 1910

The 18th. Birmingham St. Paul's Cubs in 1930

greenish colour while the first class was painted in blue, giving it more of a 'lido' effect and there was the added luxury of two towels. No-one had their own towels of course. There was also a line of 'slipper baths' and since there were no bathrooms at home, a line of men and women could always be seen queueing for them at the weekends.

Water Polo was also played and schools competed regularly in competitions like The Ansells Shield. Sometimes the pool was covered for a dance but it was learning to swim that was considered most prestigious, so crowds of kids were lined up outside the baths daily, having progressed from the breast stroke over the piano stool to being dragged the length of the pool on a pole with a loop, kicking and spluttering all the way and moving on to rubber water wings.

In those far-off days, before television and wireless, music played an important part in the life of some families during winter evenings. The type of music varied according to how poor the family happened to be. In our house, a 'pianner' would have been unthinkable and would have spent most of its life down at Mr James' pawnshop—if he took pianos in, that is. Some girls at school went home to practice on the piano for an hour before tea; we could hear them tinkling away in the front room as we clattered about in the street. (Most people who could afford a piano usually lived in a street, rather than up a terrace and had a front room.)

Our music was in the form of songs and during the Great War years, our mother would often take one of us on her knee and sing. Many of the songs seemed to be about war.

One song which I remember was a left-over from the Russo-Japanese war of 1904. Although I was only six at the time, in 1915 and the words meant nothing to me, my mind must have absorbed both words and music. The song went like this—

> "Far across the ocean, somewhere in Japan,
> Sweet little Yo san loved a sailor man.
> Sad were her daydreams, tearful was her eye,
> When that little sailor man arrived to say goodbye.
> Emperor commanded that he must join his ship,
> War was raging far and wide as to his little girl he cried
> Farewell my little Yo san, farewell my sweetheart true,
> Over the mighty ocean I've a duty there to do.
> Sometime will you remember, Toki, your sailor man,
> Who is going out to fight, for the cause of the right,
> And the freedom of dear Japan."

Another song was to illustrate her grief at losing her British soldier lover on his departure from home from Bombay, from an Indian girl.

"Will you come back to Bom-bom-bay?
Will you come back to Bom-bom-bay?
I'm grieving now you're leaving for a land so far away,
So sad and lonely I shall be all the time that you're away.
Tell me true, O tell me do, will you come back to Bom-bom-bay?

Both our Mother and Father were fond of singing and by the regularity of its rendering, their favourite song was one made popular by the well-known stage singer, Marie Kendal.

"Just like the ivy on the old garden wall,
Clinging so tightly whate'er may befall.
As you grow older I'll be constant and true,
And just like the ivy, I'll cling to you."

Another song learned from Mother, words and tune still remembered—

"While the shot and shell were screaming, upon the battlefield,
The boys in blue were fighting, their noble flag to shield.
When a cry came from their captain, "Look boys, the flag is down
Who'll volunteer to save it from disgrace?"
"I will" a young voice shouted, "I'll save the flag or die".
And he sprang into the thickest of the fray.
He saved the flag but gave his young life
All for his country' sake, they brought him back
and heard him softly say—

Ch. — "Just break the news to Mother,
She knows how much I love her,
tell her not to wait for me, for I'm not coming home,
Just say there is no other, to take the place of Mother,
Kiss her dear sweet lips for me and break the news to her".
. . .

From afar came a famous general, who'd witnessed this brave deed,
"Who saved the flag, speak up now, twas a brave and noble deed.
"The boy sir" said the captain, "is sinking very fast".
And slowly turned away to hide a tear.
The general in a moment knelt down beside the boy,

Then gave a start that touched all hearts that day.
"Tis my son, my brave young hero, I thought you safe at home".
"Forgive me father, but I ran away".

      Ch. . . .

Our grandparents lived quite near the terrace and a treasured possession of theirs was a hand-wound gramophone with a large fluted horn. This played cylindrical records of military marches and music-hall songs and when, on Sunday mornings, dressed in our best clothes, we visited our grandparents, it was not for our 'Sunday penny', welcome though it was. It was the gramophone that fascinated us. Grandad guarded it jealously and no-one was allowed to touch it but himself. He was a man of very few words, none of which I can remember, sparse as they were and his expression of possible affection was summed up in that weekly penny. I think the demonstration of emotion was deprecated by him, but Gran, clearly wanting to hug and kiss us, had to wait until we were outside the house, as she saw us on the way home.

Bicycles were still a novelty and when we had a few spare coppers, we would hire one for an hour from the little shop opposite Elkinton Street park. They cost 1½d. an hour in the early 1920's and were called 'Edie Coasters'. They had no brakes and to stop we stuck our feet on the wheel rim or dragged both boots on the ground, making the hobnails spark.

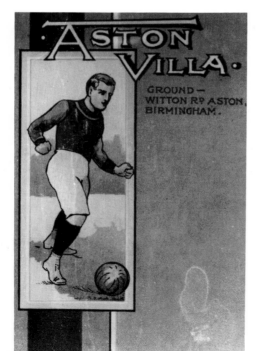

An advertisement for Aston Villa
early in the century

High Street Aston in late Edwardian times. The advert. on the side of the Hippodrome is for
Edna Latonne and Will Hay. Circus's were often held at the Hippodrome and the animals were
stabled in New Street Aston just above the Globe Picture House and after the show, elephants
and horses could be seen walking back to their 'lodgings' for the night

The Bull Ring before the first World War

CHAPTER III

Shops and Tradesmen

THERE WERE SO MANY SHOPS up the Lozells Road, on every street corner and along Aston High Street that there was really no need to go elsewhere but for we children, now a little sister as well as my brother and myself, a trip by tram to the Bull Ring was a real 'looked for' treat. Mother would get the three of us up early to catch the number 24 tram along Lozells Road, down Wheeler Street and to the terminus in Colmore Row. Then we walked through the churchyard, by the Blue-coat School, down Cherry Street, where she said there used to be a cherry orchard, and into Corporation Street and New Street.

Once at the top of the Bull Ring, the hub-hub hit us. Rows of barrows down each side of the road and in the middle spread down as far as St. Martin's — a sea of heads, barrows, horses and carts and noise. Along by the Market Hall barrow boys were packed together nearly knee-deep in rubbish. Orange boxes tripped us up, unruly potatoes bounced along the pavement and squashed tomatoes slid underfoot. There were 'Andy carrier' sellers who made us jump by yelling just as we went by and down in the middle of the Bull Ring — between the 'Ladies and Gents' and green iron railings was the man still escaping from his chains and padlocks, standing on a little peice of sacking by way of a stage and to keep the cold from striking up through the icy pavement in winter. We always stopped to watch him for a while, writhing and clanking in his padlocks. It seemed a strange way to earn a living and his boots turned up at the toes so much that a mouse could easily have sheltered under them.

Mothers dragged squalling brats along, ineffectually threatening them with dire consequences if they did not enjoy themselves—hadn't they been brought especially to enjoy themselves? Flower sellers lined the pavements, bawling "lovely violets, lovely daffs", but what we most liked were the cajoling, slick-tongued hawkers and barrow-boys who were trying to sell

Colmore Row and St. Philips

Cherry Street

New Street

The Aston Cabinet Co. in 1919, Moland Street, Gosta Green, behind what was later to be the
Central Fire Station

An advertisement for Acme Gas Stoves, made by Arden Hill and Co., at Salford Street Aston,
which was between Lichfield Road and Long Acre, by the canal

everything under the sun. There were horribly creaking balloons twisted into sausage dogs, piping hot chestnuts, cockles and winkles in little white crock dishes, goggle-eyed fish, half alive eels sliding about in trays and huge rustling crabs crawling over each other in slow motion. There were junk stalls crammed with bits of furniture, old china and old jewellery going for a few pennies but no-one up the terrace could afford to go in for those sort of luxuries. Clothes were more important and came from the cheap-jacks in the rag market or off barrows piled high with ancient frayed trousers, jerseys with the elbows out and socks with 'taters' in them. But everything could be mended and warmth, at 1d. or 2d. was more important than looking posh at 2/6. and it was surprising what a good rummage about on a stall could reveal. The 'ode stuff' as alright for playing in anyway, after all, some kids up the street had no boots even, at least not until *Daily Mail* boots appeared anyway.

The hot potato stall did a roaring trade in the winter and there was generally a little gang of urchins hanging about by his fire to keep warm. The 'Tater Man's' stall was a big black tin box on wheels with a round roof like a gypsy caravan and a quaint tall chimney with a pointed cowl sticking out of the top. There were two handles for him to shove it along the road and between them a small door which he opened every so often to poke at the little blazing fire inside. He always seemed to do this with some venom, as if angry with it and often grunted or snarled as he jabbed at the coke. Above the fire was a tray of potatoes which he continually rolled about to stop them burning. The smell of potatoes wafted around the little cart and it was not easy for tired Mothers to drag kids past the rattling spuds and aura of warmth. A ½d. bought a little triangular bagful and a spoonful of grubby salt from a sack.

The one barrow that we always used to stop at was 'the chick man's'. In the months before Christmas, his cart would be crammed with little boxes of loudly cheeping fluffy chicks surrounded by little children all pleading ''But MOM'' . . . in wailing tones. Most chicks were fed up for Christmas on scraps, such as they were. Not many folks slaughtered on the scale of the Rudds but the odd cockeral could be heard up many streets at the crack of dawn. They would frequently escape from their tiny back-yard pens and terrorize old ladies on their way to the 'lav' or find their way up an entry into the street to flutter about in a panic until someone managed to grab them. In the days when a whole chicken was nearly unheard of, these back-yard birds were highly prized as Christmas approached but we children who had carried them home in a cardboard box with holes in the side were always sorry to see them go.

J.T. Darlington, ironmonger on the corner of Bevington Road and Witton Road. Joe Darlington also had a timber business in Erdington. This Aston shop sold toys, dolls, carpets, lino, and china upstairs and a huge range of other goods downstairs. The two girls are Joe's eldest daughters — there was a younger girl, Murial — and the date is around the turn of the century

Mr E. Garland the dairyman of 181 Aston Lane near Lichfield Road with his pony and trap

As small children, it was not easy for us to struggle through the hordes of people swirling about the Bull Ring but we would plough along in the wake of our Mother as she barged along the pavement, elbows out, bags swinging dangerously and the cherries on her old black felt hat glinting in the sunlight. Once up the steps of the Market Hall the crowd seemed at its thickest in the gangways and we would come to rest in an immovable mass congregated around the china salesman who saw himself as something of an entertainer and always had the crown convulsed at his wit as he bashed the plates and cups together expertly, keeping up a continuous patter of jokes and salestalk. When we were tired of the free show we would sometimes go for a cup of tea sitting on the row of high wooden stools in the little cafe near the end of the market hall.

The most interesting shops to us were, of course, the sweet shops, when a few coppers were spare but this was rarely. After the Great War, an avalanche of goodies filled the windows after years of shortage. Liquorice came in all shapes and forms; bootlaces, thick sticks of it, pipes with red cachous on the top of the bowl. Then there were great jars of acid drops, pear drops, troach drops, pineapple drops and rock. There were great striped humbugs that suspended conversation until they dissolved, circles of peppermint rock whose sweet smell drifted out onto the pavement and beckoned us in and slabs of gleaming Williams' Milk Toffee. Like Harvino Toffee, which had crushed nuts in it, this had to be smashed with a small metal hammer by the shopkeeper. Some local shops made their own toffee, even, with figs or egg and milk flavour. Gob-stoppers, also conversation stoppers, came on sticks — the fore-runners of lollipops, then there were pink and white sugar mice with string tails.

Along Guildford Street was James Davies' and on the corner of Gower Street, George Barkers'. These were 'our' sweet shops when we lived up the terrace but we spent far more time gazing through the window than going inside. Sometimes on Saturday mornings we would hang around corner shops anyway waiting for the doorbell to ping and chorus "Got any fag cards mister?" If a man came out. Cigarette card collecting being a passion with every kid up every street resulted in this becoming the best known phrase heard throughout the country outside shop doorways.

Our Dad said that if he had a shilling for every time some kid asked him for fag cards he could have bought up the street and had enough left over for one of those new motor cars which could be seen around Handsworth. It naturally never occurred to him to contemplate moving out of Lozells.

Mrs L. Marson outside her shop in Aston Brook Street with her daughter Dorothy and grand-daughter Barbara in the 1930's. The Delicia Theatre poster advertises Sandy Powell in 'It's a Grand Old World'

The Brown Brothers advertisement for their banjo manufacturing firm at 77, Aston Road North in early Edwardian times. The workshop was near Aston Cross between the Post Office on the corner of Holland Road and the Theatre Royal

284, 282, 280, 278, WHEELER STREET,

Birmingham, *Oct 20*

RTES BOUGHT
& EXCHANGED
GOOD MAKER.

ALL NEW PIAN
GUARANTEED
YEARS. ::

CASH ONLY.

NO BRANCH

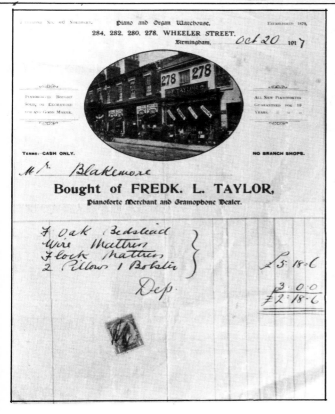

Frederick Taylor's house
furnishing shop at 278-284
Wheeler Street on the east
side of the road just above
Gerrard Street. By 1926,
ten years after this photograph, No. 284 had become
Hubert Gallagher's a
pork butcher

59

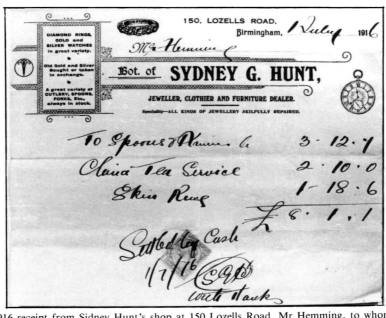

A 1916 receipt from Sidney Hunt's shop at 150 Lozells Road. Mr Hemming, to whom the invoice was addressed, was getting married and all the receipts that follow are for his house furnishings and date from the latter part of the war

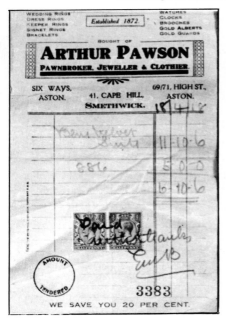

Receipts from Pawson's & Cooper's shops

60

The aristocrats of the sweets were Cadbury's and Fry's chocolate bars, advertised in white on every shop window. While we hardly ever bought these there were Cadbury's chocolate-covered walnuts at 3½d. for 4 oz. in the 20's. We would buy an ounce of these or a ½d. bar of chocolate which used up our Saturday ½d. or 1d. in one go.

There were at least two newcomers to the scene. One was a long broad brown bean and obviously from the East, it was not all that pleasant to eat but it was there and it was different and it went by the name 'Locust'. Then there was liquorice root, not connected with the black stuff but a twig from the East which could be chewed at either end to give a pungent rather acquired taste.

Since sweets were in such short supply Mother sometimes let us buy 'cocoa butter' and a tin of cocoa to make our own chocolate. The melted mixture used to set in the lids of various tins so that the round pieces of chocolate came out with names on them which we licked off first.

.. .. ..

In the years after the Great War and even into the 30's and later all deliveries were made by horse and cart or hand cart, like the woman who pushed great blocks of rock salt around Aston and stopped to saw it into small squares for us to use for cooking.

There were many milkmen who could bring a churn from the cart to the door and ladle any quantity of milk, frothing and bubbling, into a jug with a measure, and they always gave a drop extra in case some was spilt. When we lived up the terrace, we sometimes walked up to Mrs Fuller who kept the dairy in Gower Street. She wore a shining white overall and the shop was so clean that you could have eaten your dinner off the floor. The milk was served from huge buckets on the counter and you could buy a cupful of milk or one egg, if that was all you could afford, which was often the case. Mr Fullard kept his horse and trap in the yard behind the shop and went out early each morning to a farm on the edge of the city, of which there were many in those days. Once out of the rows of streets and clip-clopping along hedgerows, the pony would make frequent stops to munch real grass and save on the hay back in Lozells. When I moved to Aston, young Mr Garland in Aston Lane delivered our milk in a pony and trap with his name in fancy lettering along the side.

Radiation Ltd,
produced gas cookers
and their works
were near Aston Station

Large Scale Gas Cooking Equipment
by Radiation Ltd.

Another delivery cart was the 'Pop man' who clanked up to the door with half gallon stone jars of fizzy ginger beer and sasparilla. We really liked the glass 'pop' bottles with marbles in the top as we could smash the bottles to get at the precious 'alleys' inside but for families, the big jars were much cheaper.

Mother often sent one of us to the butchers, but not often to buy meat. We were more likely to return with half a pig's head for 3d. which she would boil and press into a china bowl with a saucer weighted down with a flat iron. This was our potted meat and made very tasty sandwiches. A bowl of faggots and peas cost 3d. as well, so sometimes we had to have a vote. Another of our favourites was the dripping we bought at 'Phillips' a la mode Beef Shop' and carried home carefully in a jam-jar. With salt and pepper on a wedge of bread, Phillips dripping was a feast and in the summer we would take it out into the yard and sit on the wall, swinging our legs and observing what was going on down the next yard. It would take something important to drag us away from our 'piece'.

One sight we did not like to miss was the rag and bone man with his goldfish. He used to shove a rusty pram around the streets with jam-jars full of fish hanging from the side swaying to and fro as the old pram bounded through horse muck and pot-holes. Even though we never had any spare clothes we liked to see the goldfish—all colours from baked bean to anaemic—slopping about in their jars. One warm September afternoon in 1925 we sat in a row on the wall munching our dripping forgetting how often our Mother could not afford to make a dinner, so we had tea for breakfast, bread and marg. for dinner and then bread and marg. with tinned tomatoes, black pudding or a bit of tripe for tea. Forgetting that we never went on holiday, rarely had a day out, that I spent each night with my brother's feet stuck under my nose since we shared opposite ends of the same bed and that we only had one winter coat between the three of us so we had to take turns in it. Phillips' dripping seemed to have this effect. Then, as we sat in the late afternoon sun, we heard the whistle going up Guildford Street which meant the rag and bone man. We slipped down off the wall and dashed up the entry, clutching our 'pieces' but of course our brother managed to drop his, nearly whole, face down on the gravel so we had to poke the goldfish to the accompaniment of his bawling which went on for so long that we had to take him home, grubby and tear-streaked. Mother found a few dried peas in a jar, though, and made him a plate of them with a sprinkling of vinegar and pepper and everything was alright again.

George Baines' Church Road, Aston, bakery shop. Best bread was 6d. for 4 pounds, the weight being made up with an extra piece if necessary, the 'make-weight', and a la mode beef was 1/- a pound. The date is around 1911

Like most folks, we rarely had a piece of real meat in the house, except perhaps late on a Saturday night when Rowbotham's and White's, the butchers up Lozells Road sold off left over meat cheaply. With the absence of freezers, meat had to be carefully watched, especially if it was none too fresh when it arrived. Bacon and ham were the most popular for those who could afford it and at the other end of the market, rotten meat was constantly trimmed off by shopkeepers and some even sold this cheaply, green, foul-smelling and reminiscent of the trenches for some. Such was the financial state of a few families.

Mother sometimes sent us all the way up to Potter's Hill to the Tripe shop. Dad was very fond of a piece of tripe, but just the look of it, lying all pale and limp in the window with flies crawling on it put us off. The rows of pigs' trotters and cows' heels looked even less promising, but once home in the pot the appetizing smell made us overlook their disembodied appearance.

64

We never had tripe at dinner-time, only sometimes for tea or supper but a real treat was three penn'orth of chips and a penn'orth of fried fish. Chip shops had blossomed forth well before the war and chips quickly became part of the working man's diet as transport for the fish improved and ice became used for preserving it.

While it was a long walk from the terrace to the tripe shop, we liked what we later realized was the atmosphere in those evenings long ago. (It was often evening when we went shopping since that was when everything was sold off cheaply). The mist-ringed shop lamps shining on caps and faces, the street swarming with people, the booming trams which were still a novelty when we were small, and then there were the smells. There used to be many little coffee shops, like 'The Ever Open Door' run by Councillor Tillotson on the corner of Alma Street and Gerrard Street. These were usually grubby stuffy little little places with steamed up windows and prices

Fred Robinson's furniture shop at 248-250 Lichfield Road, Aston around the first world war. Ten years later the premises at 248 were occupied by Thomas Storer also a furniture dealer and 250 was Thomas Adderley's cooked meat shop. The site was between Vyse Street and Grosvenor Road near Aston Station

The Midland Vinegar Company before it became H.P. sauce

THE KING'S VISIT TO KYNOCHS.

H. T. WHITLOCK & SONS. LTD
BIRMINGHAM.

The King's visit to Kynoch's

66

painted on a mirror with a bar of soap, but a tempting smell of Camp Coffee tended to lurk outside them. Tea and coffee was usually served in tumblers, scalding hot. (At home we brewed tea in Dad's tin mug and we children drank it from grey half-pound stone jam-jars with ridges down the side. Few families up the terrace had teapots or cups).

The smell from the H.P. sauce factory, once Garton's Vinegar, started by Mr E. Moore, then Midland Vinegar, filled the streets around Aston Cross, of course, and when we lived in Elkinton Street, a woman over the road who worked there reeked of onions when she passed. In the same way, anyone who worked at Ansell's carried a smell of malt with them, like our Uncle Bert who was a cooper at Ansell's.

Then, half way up New Street, Aston, at the back of some houses, was a little factory, called Dixon, Rider and Co. which crushed animal bones. Open lorries piled high with great red and white bones, trundled up their entry daily carrying a terrible overpowering stench of decay and people tended to cross the road when passing and stuff handkerchieves in their faces.

Shops, in those days, seemed far more exciting places since few foods were prepacked and everything was cut, weighed and packed as we watched and the loose food resulted in a mass of confused but delicious smells— ginger, herbs, tea, mints, smoked bacon, cheese and hessian sacks. During the Great War, rationing made butter very precious—two ounces a week— and margerine, being like cart grease was not very popular but the 'Maypole' shops sometimes had huge blocks of better quality margerine and Mother would send us dashing off up the road to join the queue, which soon formed once everyone heard about the new stock. The shop assistant would cut a pound of margerine and pat it into a neat rectangle with old ridged wooden butter pats and if we asked her she would imprint a cow on it with a butter stamp. Butter, which was known as tub butter, was cut and weighed in the same way and printed with a cow but it was not often we could afford it anyway, we just liked watching it being shaped.

Most things like tea, sugar and biscuits were all loose and packed into folded blue paper twisted into a cone with great expertise by the grocer. Even bread, usually George Baines'—was weighed and if it was short of two pounds a spare loaf was cut up for a 'make-weight', which we usually ate on the way home.

Apart from the cutting up and packing process, which made all the food shops smell so delicious, we children loved to go to large shops like W.M.

George Baines' bakery in Finch Road with some of his delivery vehicles in 1912

The No 2 flour store. All the sacks are dated 1912

The dough making room at George Baines bakery

The bread making plant

The bread ovens at George Baines' Bakery in Finch Road . No. 2 flour store

Baines' despatching department. There is a pile of trays for each of the 28 shops in the area

Taylor's at Potters Hill. Taylor's sold drapery and haberdashery and since most prices were under level money, like 11¾d, if change was required the shilling was put in a wooden container like a hand grenade, screwed on to its top half which was fixed to a pulley, a chord was pulled and away it went, rattling to the cash desk perched high in the centre of the shop. The change and receipted bill were then put in and clang, it sailed back again. There was a system of little overhead rails to each counter and we were fascinated by the containers whizzing to and fro over our heads.

On the back of this post card of the 'model bakery' the firm is writing to Mr Davies of Lodge Farm Atherstone to ask if he will send the milk by the early train the next day — December 24 1913

Gower Street School in 1923 with the staff, Messrs. Norwich, Bagnall, Evans who was the sports teacher, Faulkes and Wade

Gower Street Infants, 1926/27

CHAPTER IV

School

WHILE WE WERE ALL still living up the terrace we all started at Gower Street School, in 'the infants'. Generally late getting up we tumbled over each other rushing round to get ready. A quick cup of hot tea and tinned milk and a slide of bread and marg. then a dash up the yard to the 'lav' where there was no lock on the door so we had to keep whistling to anounce that the building was occupied, then off up the street, jam sandwiches. wrapped in last night's *Argus,* stuffed up our jerseys. We rarely had a coat and half the kids in the class had baggy jerseys from the generations of lunches shoved up them making them permanently droop in the front. The sandwiches were for mid-morning lunch as we all went back home for dinner at mid-day.

The mixed infant school was in Gower Street then my brother and I moved up to the junior school next to St. Paul's church in Lozells Road, while our sister went to Lozells Street Girls' which was further to walk so she had to set off earlier.

Our biggest problem seemed to be actually getting to school on time and we were constantly in trouble for charging in panting as the register was being called. An occasional excuse we could use was an encounter with one of the dejected little bands of cattle which we often met as they were being driven from Hockley Station to a butchers in Wheeler Street. We children were not too clear as to the difference between cows and bulls so we assumed for the purpose of safety that large bellowing animals were dangerous and would hide up an entry until they had gone by. Sometimes one would break away and canter up and down the street skidding on the muddy road and rolling its sad eyes in fear as workmen waved at it, old ladies screamed at it and crowds of the braver children scampered round it, like torreadors. It was always finally cornered in a back yard and once it had calmed down would rejoin its pals.

Exercise seemed to take up a fair amount of time at Gower street and if we were not knees bend arms stretching in the playground then it was

Gower Street Junior School in 1928. The teacher was Miss Fieldhouse

Gower Street Junior School, class V in 1934

swimming or games. On swimming mornings, Mr Cox would assemble us on the front steps of the school, each clutching a towel and costume—if we had them, otherwise they could be hired. On the signal GO we were off like greyhounds to Six Ways then up Victoria Road to the public baths, Mr Cox following us in splay-footed walk or on a number 5 tram. Mr Cox had a sadistic nature and ruled by fear. For the slightest misdemeanour in class he would approach the two-seater desk and catch hold of the offenders cheek between finger and thumb, then bringing up the other big hand he would nearly knock the child's head off. A lot of us were worried about our Dads being away during the war and even after there was a lot of deprivation so this behaviour only added to the misery.

The Gower Street playing fields were at Holford Drive at Perry Barr and on clear frosty mornings it was sheer delight to run on to lush turf, a real football at one's feet, instead of a grubby ball of tied-up rags, and dash up and down the field full of an exhilaration that sent the blood coursing.

I think that on the whole we were well-behaved, lack of hygiene, clothing and a proper diet being more notable than unruly behaviour. The visits of the school nurse (the 'nit nurse' or 'buggy nurse') were regular when she would peer at our heads armed with a carbolic soaked comb. Head lice were prone to leap quite happily and indiscrimately from one head to another so infestation was part of school life, so common that there was little real stigma attached to it, (unlike the doling out of *Daily Mail* Boots). This was particularly the case when the whole class was infested, although anyone who was really crawling would sit in splendid and self-conscious isolation with shaven head reeking of disinfectant. Soap firms assured us from advertizements on tram tickets and hoardings that their product would protect us from the dreaded bug, but in those days lots of products of a vaguely medical nature promised to cure practically everything.

Classes were large, around 50-60, and classrooms basic but most children came from cramped and overcrowded homes anyway so no-one really noticed the conditions. In any case, few of our lessons involved much movement so we spent most of our time jammed in rows of desks 'doing our tables', chanting them until they were fixed indelibly on our mind and miming when we came to the ones we could not remember, hoping the teacher would not notice. Then there were pages of sums to be laboriously copied down and worked out, poetry to be learned and strange maps to be drawn of distant lands from big red and green charts hanging on the wall. There seemed to be a lot of marching about and lining up like saluting the flag on Empire Day, too. We did P.T. in ordinary clothes; of course, most of us could barely afford those let alone a P.T. kit. Anyway, in those days,

Aston Commercial School in 1927

Albert Road School Aston early in the century. The school was between Albert Road and
Frederick Road near the back of Aston Baths. Second from the left on the middle row is Fred
Done

special kit was hardly required since knees bend arms stretch kept us rooted to the spot until our legs were wobbly.

At one time, towards the end of the Great War, I was the only boy up our end of the street who had a pair of boots and even years later, in the mid twenties, a friend of our sister's in William Street, Madge, who was the third child of six, went bare-footed until she was supplied with shoes and socks from the *Daily Mail* Fund. Since William Street was only tarmaced around 1924, this meant that Madge and many like her had to walk across rough dirt and gravel daily, not to mention the horse muck. In the late twenties, most children had shoes although possibly dropping to pieces and this being the age of the *Daily Mail* Boot there were periodic inspections at school to see who was 'needy' and eligible for free boots from the fund. Everyone dreaded being singled out and there was a lot of shuffling and embarrassment if one was even a borderline case. It was preferable to continue flapping along in second hand shoes and walking crablike through puddles, on the outer edges of ones shoes to being pointed out as 'needy'. The boots themselves even had the *Daily Mail's* initials stamped on them so that they could not be pawned, so the stigma was there constantly for all to see.

Looking around any school playground in those days there were always plenty of *Mail* outfits among the throng too. These were donated by the Christmas Tree Fund and consisted of navy blue jerseys, brown corduroy shirts, navy blue stockings and the heavy black boots. These clothes soon became a sort of uniform, informing everyone that the wearers family were poor and a lot of kids felt this keenly but most Mums were grateful at a time when new clothing was beyond their means and hand-me-downs were the rule rather than the exception. The poorest children often seemed to wear more rather than less clothes, so that a hole in one jersey was covered by the one beneath.

We seemed happy at Gower Street, we learned to sing, anyway. One song, still recalled, was sad and another was happy. This is the sad one.

> *"Come little leaves" said the wind one day,*
> *"Come o'er the meadows with me and play.*
> *Put on your dresses of red and gold,*
> *Summer has gone and the days grow cold."*

It does not seem very sad now but we thought so at the time. This is the funny one.

Lozells Street Junior School c. 1930

Lozells Street School 1932
Vera & Kathleen Lambert (Twins) Dorothy Ray, Betty Booth, Dorothy Russell, Elsie Sutton,
Maud Ure, Annie Medlam, Olive Jackson, Edna Whiteley, Jean Lutwyche, Elsie Hogg, Renee
Ellis, Edna Gavin, Winnie Nicholls, Marguerite Rogers, Doris Wyatt, Joyce Smith,
Betty Trueman—miss Morris-Teacher

A saucy cock sparrow came peeping one day,
Right into the window where we were at play.
He cocked up his feathers and tapped at the pane
And while we were watching he did it again.

At Lozells Street School, thirty-five strong and with the school motto "Nothing but the best is good enough", the discipline was strict. Miss Raines, the headmistress, lived in Lozells and actually owned a motor car, rare for anyone then, especially a woman. She was fair-minded and popular. Then there was Mrs Fox-Davies who taught geography, Miss Draper who looked after P.T., Miss McHale, Miss James, Miss Barkham, and Miss Morris who appears on the school photograph. Miss Kerr and Miss Topping taught cookery and laundry in a separate building in the playground. Miss Morris lived in Lime Grove, Lozells and Miss Barkham in Mayfield Road, Lozells. Miss James, dark-haired, small, neat and prim always wore a brown velvet dress with a lace collar.

There was an enthusiastic netball team whose motto was "Play up Lozells, get another goal gells' and on May Day a traditional May Queen and her attendants danced around a maypole, which looked remarkably like the netball post with ribbons on it. The games teacher was in charge of the dancing and the queen and her attendants wore their best white dresses, if they possessed one, with garlands of flowers around their heads.

When I was nearly fourteen years old, for reasons still obscure over sixty years later, but it was probably do do with overcrowding, I was living with our Gran in Elkinton Street in Aston and spent my last school year at Albert Road School, Aston under Mr Pilditch. Miss Butterworth was in charge of the Infants and Miss Guilder of the senior girls' school—the boys and girls were quite separate. The girls had housewifery classes in a little terraced house in Gerrard Street, Lozells, near 'the terrace' and had to march all the way from Albert Road for their lesson. I did a lot of marching about too at that time, mostly away from school, and the 'school board man' seemed to be round at Grans daily looking for me.

School was, of course, only part of our daily life, the main interest being our games in the street and in the playground. We boys played many games. While the girls skipped over and under a long rope held by a girl on each pavement, we would play for the Villa with a bundle of tied-up rags or a pig's bladder bought from the butcher for 1d. and inflated. If a lucky boy was the possessor of a real ball—a 'case-ball'—he was very popular while

In the 1925/6 season, Formans Road School won the Aston Villa Schools Cup

Aston Lane School in 1922. Mr J. Lockhart was head of the boys' school and Miss E. Jones of the girls' while Miss R. Inglis looked after the infants

the game lasted and was then consigned to mediocrity, until the next time. We had to constantly keep an eye open for 'the copper', the local policeman whom we knew by sight. The playing of football in the street was strictly forbidden. It frightened the horses.

Tip-cat was very popular up our street. The 'tip-cat' was a 3-4 inch piece of a clothes prop or broom handle whittled to a point at each end. Another piece of wood, wielded as a bat, would be chopped down smartly on one end of the 'tip-cat' which then flew up into the air and was heartily whacked into the distance by the bat. One boy had to run to retrieve it while the hitter criss-crossed the width of the street in strides. (Nothing to do with Australian trousers). The one with the highest number of strides was the winner. This, and similar games appeared to be allowed by the police but football was always a heinous crime. It seemed that no sooner had the ball been dropped in the street than a copper appeared and we had to run for it.

A popular venue of ours was the 'Old Peck', a piece of waste ground covered with cinders at the back of the 'Gothic Pub' in nearby Witton Road, We were not altogether safe from the law but with 'scouts' out we generally managed a game of some length. The lads of Aston were deprived of this spot in 1922 when the fire station was built on it.

Another pursuit was of a pyrotechnic nature. Removing the lids from empty tin-cans, we would bore holes in them, then half fill them with red hot embers from the house fire topping them up with bits of coal after first securing a loop of wire to the can. We would then swing it by the wire in front of us, fanning the coal into flames and smoke and run about the streets like dervishes leaving a trail of smoke and annoyed old ladies. We did try them out at night but were forbidden to carry one as it broke the blackout imposed to prevent the possibility of being bombed by Zeppelins. We did hear an occasional Zeppelin at night but nothing unfriendly was dropped on Aston.

One of the most popular games was whip and top which consisted of a wooden top shaped like a mushroom with a steel insert at the base on which the top spun when lashed with a whip. The awkward part was getting the thing started. We usually did this by inserting the top inbetween paving stones, wrapping the whip around it, then sending it spinning away with a flick of the wrist. This was the idea anyway but it often just flopped over and lay still. A whip and top cost ½d. each, like wooden hoops.

Frederick Road from the junction with Bevington Road looking west. The Aston Park Bakery on the corner was run by Mr S. Knight and Son

Wilson Road School in 1930. The girl in the middle with clasped hands and white collar is Margaret Eades. The school was between Heathfield Road and Birchfield Road in Handsworth but many of the pupils lived in Lozells. Note the bulging jersey on the back row. The result of having many school lunches stuffed up it in the absence of a jacket pocket.

We never had expensive toys, of course and there were no bicycles although one girl in Lozells did have a 'Fairy cycle' and we all gathered round to admire it and imagined that her parents must be very wealthy.

Marbles was a favourite game with us lads. These, some with different colours but generally plain glass from smashed lemonade bottles, were trundled along the street gutters. The idea was to bowl your marble hitting your opponents, which then became yours. Some boys used to make a 'marley machine' that consisted of a shallow lid-less wooden box, the inside of which had groups of short nails in semi-circles and numbered. At the bottom right-hand corner of the box was a spring operated lever at the top of which you were invited to place your marble and with a pull at the lever, send the marble into the box, where you hoped it would lodge in the nails. Then you would be paid off in marbles to the value of the number it carried. If your marble missed all the nails, it rolled away into the corner and was lost. Another contraption was a piece of wood like a short wooden bat, with a handle at the end. At the bottom of the bat, or 'donkey' as we called it, were cut four holes just wide enough to allow a marble to go through. The 'donkey' was held to the ground by its owner as you bowled your marble at any of the numbered holes on the same terms as the 'marley machine'.

Apart from football and cricket, the most popular street game was with the cigarette cards to be found in most packets except those which gave the silk flags that many mothers sewed into cushions. 'Skims the farthest' meant that holding the card between the fingers, you skimmed it as far as you could, probably having a dozen goes, and the winner was he whose cards were farthest from base.

We played leapfrog, while the girls hop-scotched and skipped all over the street and while we were still at school, we seldom saw that new-fangled invention the motor car but we knew most of the tradesmens' horses by name. We loved to see them take deep, suctioning gulps of water from the street troughs after their nosebags of oats had been removed.

While we lads were playing sensible games like football and marbles, the sissy girls seemed to play a lot of games involving singing. In 'Sally go round the moon' they made a circle, holding hands, first tripping round to the right and singing—

> *"Sally go round the moon, Sally go round the sun,*
> *Sally go round the chimney pots on a Sunday afternoon, WHOOPS"*

On 'whoops' they all kicked their right legs into the air and turned and

Our Football Club, Aston Villa

Aston Villa's football ground and stand in 1906 — ten years after the club's move to Villa Park. The club was started in 1874 when its ground was at Wellington Road Perry Barr

ASTON VILLA FOOTBALL CLUB.
1st DIVISION LEAGUE CHAMPIONS.   SEASON 1909-10.

Aston Villa Football Club in 1909

went the other way round. This was sung faster and faster until everyone was puffed out and fell down laughing.

"Sheep come over here' was played with every one in the game in a huddle at one end of the yard — they were the sheep. Then the 'lone wolf' stood half-way in the middle of the playground and said

> *"Sheep sheep come over".*
> *Sheep, we're afraid".*
> *Wolf, "what of?"*
> *Sheep, "the wolf".*
> *Wolf, "the wolf has gone to Lancashire and won't be back*
> *for many a year, sheep sheep come over".*

Then all the kids tore to the other end of the playground and the wolf tried to touch as many as possible. Those who were touched stayed with the wolf and helped to catch the next lot, until the one left became the wolf and the tearing up and down and wild screams started again. All very silly, but then, that was girls for you.

Another 'sissy' game was hot pennies where two teams standing in a line would pass a penny, supposed to be red-hot, down the line and the girl at the back would run up to the front and so on until the 'leader' was at the front again. The first team to sit down was the winner.

There were lots of girls' singing games such as 'Riverside' and 'In and out the Scottish Bluebells'. In 'Riverside' one girl stood in a circle of others and sang,

> *"Down by the riverside the green grass grows*
> *Where (name of the girl in the middle) washes her clothes.*
> *She sang and she sang and she sang so sweet,*
> *She called to her sweetheart across the street".*

Then a partner was chosen and they swung round in the middle of the circle singing.

> *"Sweetheart sweetheart marry me,*
> *Next Saturday afternoon at half past three.*
> *Sliced cakes, rock cakes for your tea,*
> *We'll have a jolly time at half past three.*

85

ASTON VILLA FOOTBALL GROUND, BIRMINGHAM

The Villa in action early in the century

ASTON VILLA F.C.

3831 PHOTOGRAPH OF THE ACTUAL WINNERS OF THE ASSOCIATION ENGLISH CUP, SEASON 1912-13. ROTARY PHOTO. E.C.

C WALLACE J W BACHE J LEACH J HARROP A.T LYONS H HALSE H HAMPTON S HARDY T BARBER T WESTON C STEPHENSON.

Aston Villa F.C. 1912/13

In and out the Scottish Bluebells also started with a circle, hands joined and held in the air and one girl went in and out of the circle underneath the raised arms while everyone sang,

"In and out the Scottish bluebells (repeat) my fair lady".

Whoever she stopped by she placed her hands on the girl's shoulders singing,

"Rub a dub, rub a dub on my shoulder (repeat) my fair lady".

This girl then led the first girl, holding on to her shoulder and the whole thing was repeated until no-one was left.

Then there were games like hide and seek and chalkie chase, where one team left chalk marks as clues and the other team had to find them. This was best played up the street as there were lots of terraces to hide along.

A good 'fill-in' game between football was knock and run. A little gang of my brother and I, a mate called Bashford and a few others would hang about nervously up an entry, then when no-one was in the yard, one of us would bang on the front door—there was only one door but we still called it the front door — then we would all make a rowdy get-away through the yards, over the walls and fences, all scrambling to be first, banging our knees as we went.

Organized football was the Villa, of course. Not far from the terrace was the main road leading to Villa Park. On Saturday afternoons, even before the Great War, the street erupted into noise as down swept the horse brakes, coaches with seats upstairs and down but with no roof. Crammed with supporters, some clinging to the outside of the brakes, they swayed from side to side, rattling across the cobbles with whips cracking, manes flying and all the passengers cheering. Pub customers gathered on the pavement, glasses in hand, cheering back until the whole scene resembled an up-dated sequence from Ben-Hur. If the Villa lost, the whole entourage crawled back, the horses with bowed heads and the coachmen strangely silent. So were we for five minutes. If we missed a match, the Misses Armstrong who kept a tobacconist nearby, always had the results displayed within minutes of the match ending.

One old Villa player, Billy Walton, although he was known as 'Mother', kept the Salutation Inn in Alma Street and sometimes acted as a barman at the 'Royal Oak' in Lozells Road. Our Dad used to spend hours there leaning on the polished mahogony counter listening to his tales of the old days when Aston Villa was the Wesleyan Football Club, with W.H. Price and George Ramsay as the first captains.

In the late twenties and thirties, when we were all grown up, a lot of local kids played in the Lozells Swifts in the 'Nig nog league'. This was a charity which took local children out on trips in the summer and to free 'pictures' shows in the winter as well as organizing football teams. The Swifts were run by a Mr Bunn and the father of our sister's friend, Norah.

DISTINCTIVELY DESIGNED FOR COMFORT

Burley and Sons new coach outside Witton Cemetery. Burley's garage was in William Street, Lozells

CHAPTER V

Events

In THE DISTANT DAYS of the Great War, Christmas was a real event to all of us children up the terrace. The mouth organ, penny-whistle and Jew's harp were popular instruments played by boys and nearly every boy's Christmas stocking contained a cheap tin mouth-organ. After Santa had crept back into bed, many a wakeful boy would try it out under the bed clothes until deprived of it by an irate ex Santa who had just been woken up. During the war, in the absence of fathers, mothers took over the role, often at great financial sacrifice. I remember, still aged six, my Mother taking me up to the bedroom, the 'big one', in which there was a small fire place, just before Christmas 1915. When she had previously asked me, as the eldest, what I wanted Santa to bring me I told her "a pop gun". This was a tubular affair with a cork on a string imbedded in one end that made a loud 'POP' as it shot out, pumped by a handle at the other end. "Bend down in the fire place", Mother bade me, "Tell Santa what you would like". I did so and as I finished my impassioned plea, lo and behold! Down dropped a brand new pop-gun into the hearth. Magic! Strangely enough, the matter was never referred to again, so there was no explanation of the miracle and now it is all too late of course but Mother must have attached a piece of cotton to the gun and rested it on a ledge in the chimney, given a tug and down it came. We children always had an apple and an orange in our stockings, too, plus a shiny new penny and some dolly mixtures or other sweets that were 1d. a quarter, like humbugs, liquorice allsorts, acid drops and pear drops. Stockings were emptier than today but we were still up before dawn, unwrapping our parcels in a frenzy of excitement.

One of the biggest events of the year was Pat Collin's Fair, which everyone went to on the Serpentine Ground at the back of Aston church. This fair was known as the 'Onion Fair' and was packed on Saturday nights. The ground there was covered with black ash, so by the time everyone left for home, their faces would be black too, Mums, Dads and kids alike. In the centre of the Serpentine was a pool of water, twenty feet across and

1912. Alice and Jim Poulton are leaving the Black Horse Pub in Park Lane Aston for a day trip to the countryside

Joseph and Austen Chamberlain with the Mayor and Mayoress at an Aston Hall tea party

The band stand in Aston Park c. 1905

Two anonymous Aston men around 1885 out for a jaunt in the country and photographed by
Charles & Co. of 109 High Street Aston

Pat Collins' 'Super Speedway' ride at the 'Onion Fair' on the Serpentine Ground, Aston in the 1950's. Pat Collins' fair was formerly owned by Chris Thompson from Yorkshire

George Stokes' 'Noah's Ark' at the Serpentine grounds in the 1950's

about three feet deep and once covered in ash it looked just like solid ground. The first time we took my brother and baby sister, just after the war, he, of course managed to slip away in the crowd and the next thing we heard was a loud splash nearby. He had tried to dash across the open space and promptly fell in the pool accompanied by a loud yell. He soon managed to gather quite a crowd of little, jeering kids and laughing Mums and Dads as he was dragged out by a fairground man, looking like a little 'piccaninny', black, shivering and bawling his head off.

When he was not swimming in the pond we walked round and watched the 'horses' or the cake walk, the bearded lady and the chairoplanes. One year, in the early twenties, as the chairs were spinning round on chains at their fastest, some came adrift and a number of people were flung out and killed.

At about the same time, that famous incident of the escaped lion took place, which, it seems, was witnessed by everyone who lived in Aston. I was about thirteen at the time and was holding my brother's and sister's hands as we came out of the ground, grimy, tired and mouths covered with sticky pink candy-floss. Suddenly we heard a roar from the crowd behind us and we were amazed, then excited, then terrified to see a real live lion bounding across the ground 'on the loose'. The crowd parted as if by magic as it loped in our direction. We were on the road by now, making for the tram stop but on spotting the lion, the queue scattered and the tram driver took off smartly. Old ladies in long skirts were seen sprinting along the street and people were banging on strangers doors pleading to be let in. The old lion was eventually found, toothless, bemused and waiting to be rescued on a tombstone in Aston churchyard.

Women were rarely seen in pubs in those days but children would often be sent to fetch a bottle of beer from the outdoor. Once when we were small, the vicar came just as our Gran had opened her bottle of stout. In one movement, she was up across the room and the bottle had disappeared into a cupboard. Our Dad said he had never seen her move so fast, "long black dress an' all"., We said it was a good thing that our Auntie Flossie from Elkinton Street was not there. She was too fond of 'a drop' to bother hiding it and her language was none too choice either. For this was the hey-day of the Band of Hope, when we children would be asked to sign the pledge, which we did, but mainly because we were given a shiny, new enamel brooch, or a lapel badge. Even when Dad was in the choir at St. Paul's church, he and his mates used to drop in to the pub after choir practice but Mr William Tong, the organist, spotted them one day and they were all lectured on the evils of drink and setting bad examples to the choirboys.

The opening of the Agricultural Exhibition in Aston in 1872

A sunny day in the summer of 1924. Aston's Councillor Clutterbuck's garden party

The Aston and East Birmingham C.E.
Christmas card for 1911 with W. Rodd,
J. Humphreys, E. Latham,
E. Shambrook, and T. Austin

Aston Manor Conservative Club in
Victoria Road near Six Ways.
Ernest Whitlock was the secretary
and Alfred Juggins took the photograph.
His studio was at 8 Lozells Road

95

Mr W.H. Baggs of 53 Victoria Road standing at his door during Christmas 1906. In the summer of that year the Chamberlain celebrations marked Joe Chamberlain's 70th birthday and 30 years in politics.

A labour party outing in 1925 from Lozells, probably to Clent or the 'Lickeys'

We were not too bothered about 'the evils of drink' but we did like the annual Band of Hope procession. The horses and carts were all hired from local traders and the tired old nags we knew by name in the street were transformed into gleaming new horses for a day, with plaited tails and ribbons, pulling carts decorated with coloured hoops, streamers and trimmings. The dull old streets became a blaze of colour as at mid-day all the side-streets spilled into Lozells Road with cowboys and very red Indians, small nurses and missionaries, cardboard Roman soldiers with deadly wooden swords and delicate fairies with wire and paper wings. Then the laden carts were organized into some sort of order and at a given signal, off they all went. (The tableaux themselves were all domestic scenes of drunken fathers and cowering children contrasted with happy families who did not drink). First up to Bendall's corner ('High Class Confectioner') with its huge clock on the building and the procession wheeled round to the right into Hamstead Road, a great contrast to our dreary Lozells streets.

White bonneted maidservants cheered from doorsteps and waved feather dusters, trams clanged and upstairs passengers leaned over the rail to shout

The Lake, Victoria Park, Handsworth, circa 1910

97

Labour party supporters in Lozells c. 1925

Out with the labour party in 1926. Everyone is mostly from the William Street area of Lozells

encouragement as the mob swung noisily down the hill, into the dip to the gates of Handsworth park. Then turning left through the gates it passed the boating lake, complete with swans, island and boats full of self-conscious young men showing how they could feather an oar, in case any girls might be looking on.

At the far side of the park on the high meadow, by the Grove Lane entrance, everything came to a halt. Horses were gratefully unharnessed and taken away to a corner of the meadow for nosebags and water and left to their own devices. Excited children were unshipped, scrubbed trestle tables laid out and stacked with sandwiches, cakes, great gleaming tea urns and huge brown enamel tea pots and then the sports began. This was the usual sort of thing, with the fifty yard dash, egg and spoon race and sack races but with the added interest of many children being in fancy dress, so cowboys dropped their guns in mid race and had to go back for them, crying, soldiers tripped over their swords and fairies' cardboard wings fell off in all the pushing and shoving at the start.

All the while there was further excitement from trains steaming through the park with passengers leaning out of the carriages and cheering and everyone was aware of the cameraman with his big mahogony and brass plate camera. He was a regular visitor and the slides were shown at the Lozells Picture House during the next week so everyone could shriek with laughter at themselves even though the only sound was the pianist tinkling away on the piano. This, of course, was long before the age of the cinema.

Late in the afternoon, the whole procession formed up again, still collecting crowds and cheers along the streets returning home until back at Wheeler Street, parents reclaimed tired, dusty children and gleaming colourful steeds became the milkman's carthorse again.

Another exciting time was 'the elections'. There was no television or radio, of course, so candidates tramped around the streets, stopping on the corners and started spouting on an orange box, soon gathering a crowd. We children could never grasp what they were shouting about but it was great fun when the rotten tomatoes started flying. On election day itself, 'followers' were very important to add volume to the crowd and we were more than happy to race after any lorry or horse and cart that would give us a ride round the streets sporting the appropriate rosette shouting our heads off and, of course, sucking the sweets dished out to get us cracking. We did not care which party we were representing, but happily roared out 'vote vote vote for . . . he will sure to win the day. If you vote for any other he will put you in the gutter, vote vote vote for . . .'

The reconstruction of Aston Bridge on Sunday March 25 1906. The post card tells us that the new bridge was placed in position in 15½ minutes

FRIENDSHIPS GREETING

Only a picture post-card
To you we send this year
And though without color or tinsel
Our message is just as sincere

May the joys and the goodwill
              of Christmas

Abundantly enter your doors
May the New Year be blessed
           with few sorrows
Is our wish unto you and
              to yours

FROM
Cllr. & J. Pearsall
7 WITTON ROAD
  SIX WAYS
    ASTON   1903.

Mr & Mrs Pearsall's Xmas Card from Witton Road, Aston

One very happy day was the Silver Jubilee of King George and Queen Mary. Every house down the street was festooned in red, white and blue and for most of us small children it was the first time we had experienced anything like the joy of walking through the garlanded streets. On Jubilee day, we all got up early and joined a gang from the youth club and partly by tram — sitting on top of course to see the view and the sparks from the trolley head — and then walking, we got to Clent where we raced about over the hills all afternoon. Later, we sat on the top of the hill and had our bread and dripping and bottle of water, looking at the pall of smoke over Birmingham and wondering what it was like in the distant blue haze towards what we were told was Shropshire and then Wales. Did kids there have bread and scrape? We had heard that everyone in the country kept a pig, so we thought they must all be very rich if they could afford to feed a pig as well as themselves. Once it became dusk the great bonfire was lit and flames shot high into the air as the huge pile of wood slipped now and then causing pops and bangs that made us jump and clouds of sparks to shower around. We stood strangely silent in this new, magical place for we had never been on a hill before with the wind roaring in our ears in the dancing red glow of an enormous bonfire watching the dull glow of Birmingham and home in the distance. But with increasing hunger the spell was broken and we dashed back down the hill in the gathering gloom and set off for home.

Once in Lozells we passed one street party after another en route for the terrace, so with a song here and a dance there we eventually made it back home just in time to rescue a few sandwiches and bowls of strawberry jelly from the clutches of kids from other streets who were dropping in at everyone elses party for 'seconds'. Then later in the evening we all trooped down to Aston Hall for the grand firework display which was even more exciting and memorable than when the R101 airship went over our school and we were all allowed to run out into the playground to watch it.

A post card posted in October 1904 entitled 'Behind Aston Church' and sent to a Miss M. Proctor with the message "Just sending this to say how I love you"

CHAPTER VI

War

As THE WAR ENTERED its most vicious phase with battles at The Somme, Ypres and Passchendaele, the number of people around Lozells wearing black armbands as symbols of loss increased enormously. This was not surprising in retrospect when we read in the paper that as many as 60,000 dead and wounded were recorded in one battle. In one day.

To many homes in the street came the dreaded War Office telegram beginning 'The War Office regrets to inform you . . .' Mother must have been very anxious about Dad but of course, we three kiddies were too busy with our games to notice such emotion. For a graphic realization of what war looked like, magazines, read at the library in Witton Road ran a collection of artists' impressions of battle scenes; bombs dropping, shells exploding among men and horses, soldiers hanging on barbed-wire entanglements. They were in *The Sphere* and *London Illustrated News* and the best were by an artist called Alberto Matarnia. Dad was somewhere in The Balkans, in Greece and Bulgaria actually, but Mother still worried nevertheless. Then suddenly, one day, my grandparents received a telegram. My uncle Walter, then only eighteen years old had been killed with the Artillery in the Dardanelles. He was my Mother's youngest brother and when he left home he promised me a donkey on his return. While there was much grief at all the loss of such young life, a quiet sense of the inevitability of it all was accepted by most people. Then, when seventeen year old Uncle Harold was killed at Passchendaele, somehow it did not seem so shocking.

By the middle of the war I was six years old and had begun to notice that fathers, uncles and brothers were disappearing from homes. When our Father had gone away I remember Mother crying and holding me to her and saying something about a war. "What's war?" I asked. She told me it was a place where men were unkind to each other and held me tightly. We two boys drew nearer to her in an uncomprehending desire to be close and our baby sister slept in her arms.

Aston Park Gates. The Park Road entrance with Aston church in the background. The photograph was taken by George Lewis, a well-known publisher of post cards in Acocks Green and as it is an early picture of his — he started photographing in Birmingham in 1904 — we can see work starting on the tramway in Park Road which was opened in the same year

I had started school, Gower Street Infants, a year before and our teacher Miss Withey asked the class whose father had gone to war. Nearly all hands shot up at which Miss Withey looked nicely at us and shook her head slowly. I wondered if, perhaps, they had been naughty to go. I would not have gone anywhere to be treated unkindly.

At the end of our terrace was a brick wall and on it, in Guildford Street, there appeared one day the face of a soldier with a big moustache, who, pointing a finger at me, appeared to be saying something. I could not read the print at the end of his finger so I asked a woman passing by what it was. She smiled, patted me on the head and said, "he doesn't mean you son, he wants men to become soldiers. That is General Kitchener". I was glad he did not want me. He looked so cross that I was worried about having got my plasticine stuck in another boy's hair at school the boy's mother, Mrs Turner, could have told him although I had already been punished by a slap on the bottom from Miss Withey.

As the war progressed, our standard of living, such as it was, began to be affected by the economic situation. Prices of some food increased when it became available and long queues were a frequent sight up the Lozells Road. The total income of our family was only a few shillings a week and we often sat in the winter's gloom with candles taking over from the gas mantle because a penny in the gas meter meant no bread or milk. Items of jewellery belonging to Mother began to disappear and could be seen later through the pawnbroker's window. Clothing, such as Dad's best suit were resting there also, more permanently this time, carefully folded on his

The old stocks in Aston Park

'Win the war day' at Kynochs amunition factory at Witton. Although outside Aston, a lot of Aston men and women worked there, especially during the war

shelves with mothballs for company. There was absolutely no chance, under the conditions existing then, of them ever being redeemed and wounded servicemen coming home often found that they no longer had a civilian suit to wear. Having known the adequacy of stews and bully-beef in the army they did not initially understand the struggles and anxieties housewives were facing daily in their efforts to survive. Most Mothers neglected themselves as long as their children had something to eat and dinner for some kiddies was a penny bar of chocolate eaten on the way back to school.

At home, signs of the war were appearing even to us children. One day, the street grapevine told us that a Zeppelin had been shot down over Wednesbury and that the debris had been taken to our own Victoria Square and were on show there. There was a mad dash for the number six tram to Martineau Street after school and hundreds of boys and adults poured into town to see a tangible part of the war. The remains of the airship lay in a fragmented heap alongside the townhall, a tangled mass of aluminium-

Church Lane Aston c. 1914

JUBILEE BELLS, ASTON PARISH CHURCH

1935. The new bells have arrived, commemorating the Silver Jubilee of George V and Queen Mary, 1910-1935

Albert Road and the junction with Upper Thomas Street. The delivery card belongs to
CAMWAL LTD — aerated water manufacturers at Cheston Road, Aston

St. Paul's Church Lozells Road

St. Paul's Church.
— interior

The old Aston Cross which was demolished in 1891

coloured metal that had formed the skeletal framework. We gazed at the wreckage in awe, our young, fertile imaginations busily conjuring up its flight from Germany, across the North Sea and daring to come so far inland. Although the area was roped off, several people managed to pick up pieces as souvenirs.

Then, after battles in France, the sight of walking wounded became common. They were allowed out on weekend passes and wore conspicuous light blue coats and trousers, white shirts and red ties and quite often they were invited into private homes for a meal.

Up the terrace, neighbours would gather to discuss the latest crop of War Office telegrams and their recipients, their voices muted at the realization that more well-known faces would not be returning to the street while bereaved children played near them quite unconscious of the fact that they had suddenly become fatherless, until they saw their mother's tears. Most of the women wore shawls and often mens' cloth caps but when there was a loss in the family the cap was exchanged for the emblem of widowhood, the bonnet tied under the chin with black ribbon or velvet.

The folks in the terrace seemed to grow closer during the war — the Toveys, Lights, Colemans, Kendals, Greys and Lings. Then on the other side was Mrs Frogatt, the Browns and Hindles. The Lights had a daughter, Bessie, and three sons and like me, when I went to live with our Gran in Elkinton Street, Bessie had to live with a relative as there was not enough space for more than two or three children in those cramped little houses. Not grown-up ones anyway, and she was the eldest child. Mrs Crump was

Witton Road showing Aston Library

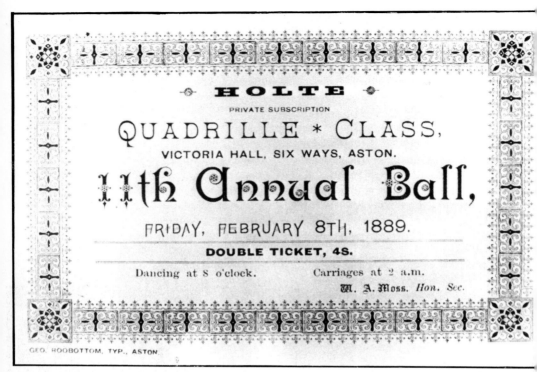

A double ticket, costing 4/-, for the Holte private subscription Quadrille class at Victoria Hall

the character of the terrace. She knew just one song, the old Victorian ballad 'Thora', and she belted it out daily with everyone awaiting the top 'C' which she put in the rendering herself. She never made it but had many valiant attempts. Neighbours swore that the hens alway stopped laying when she was 'on song'.

By 1918 I was able to read the *Mail and Despatch* and became well informed on the progress of the war and could follow the events which might involve our Dad. Then, suddenly in November, the church bells began to ring, peal after peal. People rushed into the streets cheering and shaking each others hands while women sang and factory bulls (hooters) blared away like muffled bassoons. Parties were arranged on meagre rations and bunting appeared as if by magic to decorate the street. We had a day off school to celebrate the armistice and even our street games were forgotten in the euphoria of victory as the nation sat and awaited the homecoming of our heroes.

Then, to tumultous welcomes, they began to arrive. Snow Hill and New Street Stations were thronged with hundreds of people anxiously looking for familiar faces in the sea of khaki. One day, Mother seemed to be more light-hearted than of late. She told us that there might be a pleasant surprise later that day but would not say what. I wondered if mine might be a mouth-organ and went off to school. Later than day, I was playing football during playtime in the playground when a soldier approached me. He stopped at my side, looked down at me, smiled and said gently, "Hello son". Looking up at him I gasped "Dad!" I clung to him with sudden unexpected tears in precious, never to be recaptured moments. He took my hand and said "Come on son, lets go home". And we did.

The aftermath of war brought many innovations, one of the most noteworthy being the arrival of the army greatcoat, brass buttoned and half

Aston Hall c. 1901

1906 Post Card of cat fostering chicks — Simpsons, Aston

POST CARD.

A STRANGE FOSTER-MOTHER.

A striking example of the manner in which predatory habit is subjugated by maternal instinct has been furnished by a cat, belonging to Messrs. W.H. Simpson and Sons, Corn Dealers, of High St., Aston, which has become the foster-mother of five recently-hatched chickens. The foster-mother is getting on in years, and it is about eighteen months since she had a family of her own. Hitherto this particular cat has been chiefly distinguished as an exceptionally good mouser. She has now proved that she can protect as well as she can destroy, and her adoption of the chickens was purely spontaneous. The chickens, artificially incubated, has been sent to be exhibited as an advertisement by the manufacturers of a poultry food. When they arrived they were placed near the fireplace in the office, where the old cat was sleeping in a hamper. Attracted by the chirping of the new visitors, the cat came out to see what was the cause of the unusual noise, and her maternal instinct being aroused by the resemblance of the downy coats of the little strangers to the soft furry covering of her last litter of kittens, she gently scooped them with her paw into her sleeping place, and covered them with the same tender care as if they had been her own offspring. The chickens seem to have taken very well to their foster-parent, though they were a little disconcerted at first when the cat began to wash them. This is a regular part of the day's duties of the foster-mother, and her children have now become quite accustomed to it, though it proved fatal to one of the chickens, who was in a very weakly condition when it arrived. The cat is a very devoted mother. She followed the chickens when they were removed to the window, and never leaves them excepting for a short period when she takes her own food.

Birmingham Mail, May 12th, 1906.

114

belted. These coats had lain, together with their wearers, in the muddy hell of the Somme and other battlefields and were now brought home to become an extra blanket on the bed. In some cases they were worn by their owners during the day, in search for work and to show that they had 'done their bit'. Ours was the only house in the terrace to have one, Dad being the only Father to go to war, but he never wore it since it became our quilt. It became the butt of many a joke such as when parents were entertaining visitors one evening, their two young children having been put to bed and the conversation was interrupted by a cry from upstairs that Dad's army coat had slipped off the bed. Flustered, the Mother went upstairs, replaced the wayward coat, and told the kids "you must not call it a coat, it's a quilt". Some minutes later, another call rang out. "Mom? Jimmy's got his foot stuck in the sleeve of the quilt".

After the war, mothers who had worked on munitions and who had husbands in reserved occupations, found their incomes halved once they returned to being housewives and short time working and unemployment were common. On the other hand, grocers, butchers and greengrocers were able to employ boys to deliver orders now that food supplies were available again and young lads on bicycles fitted with carrier frames containing huge wicker baskets attached to the handle bars were a common sight. The bicycles usually had a tin plate fixed to the frame on which was painted the name of the shop. Butchers always added 'Purveyor of meat' after their name. Boys worked at these jobs half time, after school and all day Saturday.

Aston and Lozells had many corner shops shown as 'hucksters' which had once been ordinary houses but which had been converted to sell a variety of commodities like sweets, groceries, firewood, candles, gas mantles, bootlaces and buttons. In most of these shops there was a 'tick' system where customer would take their goods away but pay at the end of the week. Most shops carried bad debts as a result of this system and thought it did not exist as such, in the middle-class residential areas like Handsworth, even there, payment of bills was often slow and still folks sent in their orders.

Another part time job for boys was that of 'lather boy' in a barbers shop. Their task was to prepare the customers face for shaving by the barber. Most men grew two or three days stubble so that when the boys rubbed the bristles, they felt like gramophone needles and it was only about three or four days before the boy's hand was so grazed that he had to give up the job. The razors were cut-throat of course, and customers kept their own shaving mugs at the shop. These were crock and often had on them flower motifs and the owners' initials. The style of hair-cut was generally 'short back and sides' and long moustaches came in for cosseting with pomade to stiffen them a la Kaiser.

I was now 14 years old and one morning in the summer of 1923 I set off with my Dad for my first job in Miller Street, Aston, making transformer moulds. As we strode down the street in the early morning haze, sandwiches wrapped in the *Sports Argus* and stuffed in our pockets, I looked back at the terrace. A few children were kicking a can about further up the street and a delivery horse stamped impatiently at the end of Bright Terrace. Everything looked much as it had a decade earlier. It began to dawn on me that childhood was over.

Aston Cross before the first World War

Aston Hall, circa 1910

The Clergy House, Aston

LOCAL BOOKS
by local authors

THE ROYAL TOWN of SUTTON COLDFIELD
A Commemorative History
by Douglas V. Jones

Running to 208 pages and covering the period from Saxon times up till 1974, when the Royal Town of Sutton Coldfield was amalgamated with Birmingham this is a warm human story of local people, events and landmarks.

SUTTON COLDFIELD 1974-1984 The Story of a Decade
by Douglas V. Jones

A lavishly illustrated Chronicle which recalls the many changes to the face of Sutton since its merger with Birmingham, with a Pictorial Supplement, *Sutton in 1984.*

SUTTON PARK Its History and Wildlife
by Douglas V. Jones

Profusely illustrated with a wide selection of old and new pictures most of which have not previously been published, complete with centrefold map, and detailed with three interesting walks short enough for the casual walker to take at leisure.

STEAMING UP TO SUTTON How the Birmingham to Sutton
Coldfield Railway Line was built in 1862
written by Roger Lea

Every day thousands travel on the railway line between Sutton and Birmingham, without giving much thought to its origins and history. This is the fascinating story.

MEMORIES OF A TWENTIES CHILD
by Douglas V. Jones

A nostalgic trip into one man's childhood and youth during the years between the wars. The book is a profusely illustrated reminder of the age of steam, gas-lamps, crystal-sets and tramcars.

DURATION MAN 1939-46 My War
by Douglas V. Jones

An enthralling sequel to "Memories of a Twenties Child"

This is the story of some of those who fought the good fight against red tape, boredom and gloom in places where all three were often present. If from time to time it may appear that soldiering is a mug's game, then the reader must draw his own conclusions. 144 pages, fully illustrated.

ROUND ABOUT THE ROTUNDA Four Decades of Life in and
around Birmingham 1945-1987
by Douglas V. Jones

This sequel to *Memories of a Twenties Child* and *Duration Man* presents an enthralling and evocative picture of Birmingham in transition during the last four decades reminding us on the way of the many interesting landmarks which have now disappeared. Illustrated with over a hundred photographs of the passing scene.

THE STORY OF ERDINGTON
From Sleepy Hamlet to Thriving Suburb
by Douglas V. Jones

Tracing the history of Erdington from earliest times, through the ages up to the late twentieth century. With ninety-eight illustrations including a period map circa 1880.

EDGBASTON As It Was
by Douglas V. Jones

Edgbaston is no ordinary suburb. Phrases such as 'a rural oasis' and 'Britain's finest 19th century suburb' have been used to describe it. But Edgbaston has more than beauty to commend it. It is a place steeped in history and this book delves into its colourful past and the people who have shaped it.

THE BOOK OF BRUM or 'Mekya Selfa Tum'
by Ray Tennant

Ramdom thoughts on the dialect and accent of the Second City (Brumslang) with a glossary of the most common expressions plus Brumodes, Brumverse and Brumericks with a little more serious verse. Brilliantly illustrated with cartoons by Jim Lyndon.

A SECOND BOOK OF BRUM Aware Din Urea
by Ray Tennant

Further thoughts on the dialect and accent of Birmingham with a glossary containing many sayings of historical interest plus a little more verse and cartoons by Lyndon. Many expressions from the past are included in this Second Book of Brum.

Last Tram Down The Village and Other Memories of
YESTERDAY'S BIRMINGHAM
by Ray Tennant

Although all the places written about are centred in or very near Birmingham it will, hopefully, be of interest to people who live in other cities since many of the memories could be shared and appreciated by anyone who lived through the traumatic years of the thirties and forties.

SOLID CITIZENS Statues in Birmingham
by Bridget Pugh
with drawings by Anne Irby Crews

Presenting a collection of illustrations and accounts of some of the main figures to be found in the city. Together they represent the history of Birmingham and those associated with it during the last thousand years.

A FEAST OF MEMORIES Black Country Food and Life at the Turn of the Century
by Marjorie Cashmore

Marjorie Cashmore has worked at The Black Country Museum in Dudley for the past ten years and has in that time amassed a wealth of recipes and information on The Black Country, its people and its food. All this, supplemented by her own upbringing and family history, has been vividly recorded in this absorbing book. *Profusely illustrated.*

UP THE TERRACE Down Aston and Lozells
by Ronald K. Moore

A fascinating account of life in the back streets of Birmingham before, during and after the first World War. With over 120 illustrations that effectively capture the atmosphere of the period.

Obtainable from Bookshops or direct from:

Westwood Press Publications

44 BOLDMERE ROAD, SUTTON COLDFIELD, WEST MIDLANDS
Telephone: 021-355 5268

Illustrated Book List available on request. (Additional titles are constantly added).